RELIGION IN LIFE CURRICULUM
Edited by Edward A. Fitzpatrick, Ph.D.

FIRST GRADE TEACHERS PLAN BOOK
AND MANUAL

BOOK OF THE HOLY CHILD (Grade One)

LIFE OF MY SAVIOR (Grade Two)

LIFE OF THE SOUL (Grade Three)

BEFORE CHRIST CAME (Grade Four)

THE VINE AND THE BRANCHES (Grade Five)

THE MISSAL (Grade Six)

HIGHWAY TO GOD (Grades Seven and Eight)

Accompanying this Series is the RELIGION
IN LIFE CURRICULUM for grades one
to six and PRACTICAL PROBLEMS IN
RELIGION for grades seven and eight.

Religion in Life Curriculum

First Grade Teachers Plan Book and Manual

Designed for use with the
HIGHWAY TO HEAVEN SERIES
of Catechism Textbooks

ST. AUGUSTINE ACADEMY PRESS
HOMER GLEN, ILLINOIS

Nihil obstat:
    H. B. RIES,
        Censor librorum

Imprimatur:
    ✠ SAMUEL A. STRITCH,
        Archiepiscopus Milwaukiensis

June 16, 1934

This book was originally published in 1934 by The Bruce Publishing Company.

This edition reprinted in 2018 by St. Augustine Academy Press.

ISBN: 978-1-64051-002-9

EDITOR'S FOREWORD

This is the Teacher's Plan Book and Manual for the first grade of the Religion-in-Life curriculum. A textbook, *The Book of the Holy Child*, to be placed in the hands of the child is the organized material for the child as this is for the teacher.

The Religion-in-Life curriculum is an effort to bring to bear on the fundamental problem of education, the teaching of religion, the sifted insight of the ages and the best pedagogical procedures of our own day.

The teacher should acquaint herself thoroughly with the underlying plans and procedures of the Religion-in-Life curriculum.* This can be done most directly by securing a copy of the curriculum from your diocesan superintendent or your community supervisor (or from the publisher, The Bruce Publishing Company, Milwaukee, Wisconsin). Study its introduction as a statement of the ultimate objectives each teacher in each room must be aiming at and helping to secure. Study the general statement of the work of your own grade. Look at the work of the succeeding grades to see what foundations you must lay for this later work. If you will do this, you will realize as perhaps you will in no other way the unified, cumulative, progressive character of this organized effort to make religion a factor in man's present life for his eternal welfare. So far as knowledge is concerned, it is "an approach through the mind of man to the will of man," in Archbishop Murray's fine phrase.

We welcome suggestions from any teacher who uses this manual. It will be a service to thousands of Catholic children in their supreme life interest. This curriculum, the textbooks, and manuals have only one excuse for being: to help Catholic children attain eternal salvation. We ask your coöperation to make them even better than they are.

---

* Pertinent pages from this master curriculum manual, entitled "A Curriculum in Religion," have been included in this volume in excerpted form, and can be found on page xii.

Many parents and Sisters have coöperated in this and in the former teacher's plan book and manual. We are grateful, indeed, to all of them.

In offering this Manual, we are keeping faith with the teachers who are using the Religion-in-Life Curriculum. We shall continue to study the problems involved, and as more extensive experience is fruitful of better techniques and better organization of material they will be made available to teachers. We repeat our earnest request that, if you in your classroom experience develop any methods or practices or devices that may help other teachers serve Catholic children better, you would send them to us at the Catechetical Institute, Marquette University.

Edward A. Fitzpatrick

EDITOR'S NOTE TO THE REPRINTED EDITION:

In reassembling this *Religion in Life Curriculum*, we thought it best to include excerpts from the curriculum overview volume, titled *Curriculum in Religion*, which was published in 1931 as the basis for development of the fleshed-out Teachers Plan Book and Manual before you. In that original volume, the entire curriculum for first through eighth grades were laid out in basic outline form, with attention given to the main focus, goals and resources for each grade. You may find that some of the resources listed in these excerpts did not find their way into the current manual. However, we felt it would be helpful to the teacher (or parent) to see a summary of the intended vision for the current year.

In the appendix found at the rear of this volume, we have also provided a comprehensive listing of all the recommended resources found in this manual, to which we have added notations showing the most frequently used and/or most helpful resources, as well as those which can be found online.

Lastly, please note that most of the recommended student readings (that is, those which would have been found in the various school readers listed throughout this book) have been assembled and printed under one cover in the new *Magnificat Readers* which accompany this series.

Lisa Bergman

St. Augustine Academy Press
February 2018

ACKNOWLEDGMENTS

Grateful acknowledgment is made for the advice and the assistance given by capable and experienced groups of teachers in the Northwestern Province of the School Sisters of Notre Dame; and especially to the teachers of SS. Peter and Paul's School, Mankato, Minnesota, who gave these Units experimental trials in the classroom.

CONTENTS

ix

The following section is an excerpt from the book "A Curriculum in Religion," included for the convenience of teachers as a way of familiarizing themselves with the basic goals laid out for the Religion in Life Curriculum for the First Grade.

RELIGION IN GRADE I

Main Interest: The Childhood of Christ

FOR the tots who are in the first grade, the main objective is to give the child the fullest possible knowledge on this level of the Christ Child. Consequently, the texts of the year should deal definitely with the childhood of Christ. Love of the Christ Child is more important at this stage than any knowledge of doctrine. Interest in the Christ Child is more useful in every way than the memorization of all the answers in the Catechism.

As far as possible, everything in the grade should grow out of the story of the childhood of Christ. If a patron is to be selected for this grade it should obviously be the Christ Child. The idea of the patron might be permitted to wait until Christmastide, and then have the children suggest it.

Outline of Main Topics

In the first semester the child will be learning reading, using secular material. Teachers will give only oral instruction in religion in the first semester. The material should include the stories listed below in oral form, acquainting the pupils with the essential vocabulary with main interest around the birth of Christ, culminating in the celebration of Christmas.

In the second semester the child will read from his text or texts or find in supplementary readers the following stories regarding the childhood of Christ:

1. God, the Creator of Heaven and Earth
2. Angels
3. The Announcement to Zachary
4. The Birth of John
5. The Annunciation to Mary
6. Mary's Visit to Elizabeth
7. (Nativity) Jesus is Born
8. The Shepherds Seek Christ
9. The Wise Men Adore Christ
10. Christ is Brought to the Temple
11. The Flight into Egypt
12. The Return to Nazareth
13. Christ in the Temple
14. The Holy Family

Text: Basal and Supplementary

The Basal Text for the course is Sister Bartholomew's *The Book of the Holy Child* (Bruce). The Supplementary Text designed especially to supplement the foregoing is Berdice Moran's *The Childhood of Christ, Verse for Tiny Tots* (Bruce).

Activities

The following activities will be carried out in connection with the above stories:

Clay modeling — the crib; sheep.

Paper cutting — angel; sheep; doves; dove cage; palm trees; booklet; covers.

Poster making — Christmas star; camels; Nazareth; Bethlehem.

Sand-table construction — The cave at Bethlehem; shepherds on the hillside; village of Nazareth; workshop of Joseph; desert scene.

Story-telling — Oral talks on things God has made; What I saw in heaven; What I saw in the Temple; What was said in the Temple; How Jesus spent His day, etc.

Booklet making — Of angel pictures; of pictures of the childhood of Jesus.

Dramatization — The message of the angel; the arrival of the shepherds.

Written Work — Simple sentences in booklets.

Preparation for Holy Communion

The preparation for Holy Communion undertaken in this grade should conform to the fine wisdom and insight of Pius X in that extraordinary document, the *Decree on Early Communion,* (approved Aug. 8, 1910. See also decree of Dec. 20, 1905). The teaching and preparation should be inspired by the spirit and words of the saintly Pope. The substance of the decree is as follows:

The age for the reception of Holy Communion is "the age of discretion," the age at which the child begins to use its reason, that is, about its seventh year, or later, or even sooner.

The determination of when the child is to receive Holy Communion is in the hands of parents and confessor.

The child must be able to understand "according to its capacity": The truth of the Holy Trinity; the Incarnation of God the Son; the death on the cross for our redemption; God is the rewarder of the good and the punisher of the wicked.

As regards the Blessed Sacrament, it is enough if the child "distinguishes the Eucharistic bread from common and material bread so as to approach the Holy Eucharist with such devotion as befits its age."

All those in charge of children must "take the utmost care that after their First Communion the said children should approach the holy table very often, and, if it be possible, even daily, as Jesus Christ and our Holy Mother Church desire it, and that they do so with such devotion of soul as their age allows."

The attention of pastors and teachers is especially called to the phrase "according to its (child's) capacity," as "befits its age," or as "their age allows." The preparation for Holy Communion is not the final study of the Catechism.

The content for this preparation which will often be undertaken by the pastor himself will be found in Father William R. Kelley's, *First Communion* (Benziger), which is recommended as a text. This work when undertaken in this grade should come in the second semester.

Poems

The following poems should be presented orally by the teacher or read from texts or mimeographed sheets.

  *1. *The Creation*, Berdice Moran,
  *2. *The Creator*, John Keble,
   3. *I Wish I Could See the Bright Angel*,
  *4. *Beautiful Angel*, Anonymous,
   5. *When Little Children*, Anonymous,
  *6. *The Annunciation*, Anonymous,
  *7. *Good Night*, Father Tabb,
  *8. *Out of Bounds*, Father Tabb,
   9. *Christmas*, Anonymous,
  10. *Like One I Know*, Nancy Campbell,
  11. *Christmas Night*, Father Faber,
  12. *Christmas Carol*, Sara Teasdale,

   13. *Gifts,* Julia Johnson Davis,
  *14. *Gifts,* Christina Rossetti,
  *15. *A Little Child at the Crib,* Rev. Wm. Ennis,
  *16. *Jesus Answers from the Crib,* Rev. Wm. Ennis,
  *17. *A Little Boy's Gift,* Hope Cecil,
  *18. *A Song,* Charles L. O'Donnell, C.S.C.,
  *19. *The Birds,* Hilaire Belloc,
   20. *Our Lord and Our Lady,* Hilaire Belloc,
   21. *Little Jesus,* Francis Thompson,
  *22. *Nazareth,* William Doyle, S.J.,
  *23. *Hide and Seek,* Father Tabb,
  *24. *A Mother's Quest,* Hugh Francis Blunt.

The simpler poems should be taken up in the first
half of the year orally, by the teacher, and the most
difficult ones could be similarly taken up at the end
of the year, which will serve as a preparation for the
later study. There should be throughout the course
continual recurrence to these poems. At least the
poems starred should be memorized. All should be
memorized if time permits. The children should have
as a text for the poems: *Religious Poems for Children*
(*Primary Grades*) (Bruce).

Picture Study

The children should know the following pictures,
which should be presented in connection with the
stories studied. Some should be made a matter of special study:

   1. The Guardian Angel — Plockhurst,
   2. Guardian Angel — Guercine,
   3. Annunciation — Titian,
   4. Annunciation — Andrea del Sarto,
   5. Annunciation — Bouguereau,
   6. Adoration of the Shepherds — Murillo,
   7. Arrival of the Shepherds — Lerolle,

8. Adoration of the Magi — Durer,
9. The Presentation — Vittore Carpaccio,
10. Flight into Egypt — Plockhurst,
11. Repose in Egypt — Plockhurst,
12. Repose in Egypt — Van Dyck,
13. Christ in the Temple — Hoffmann.

Aspirations of Brief Prayers

As opportunity offers, the following aspirations or others will be taught. One might be selected and written on the board each month, calling attention to it as opportunity permits. The students might prepare aspirations of their own.

1. Jesus, Mary, Joseph,
2. Jesus, Mary, Joseph, I give You my heart and soul,
3. Hallowed be Thy name,
4. Infant Jesus, bless us,
5. Blessed be God.

Prayers

1. The Hail Mary should be taught in connection with the Annunciation.

2. The Our Father, which many of the children will have heard or know partially, should be taught as the prayer which the Christ Child Himself taught when He became a man.

3. The Angelus might possibly be taught (orally) as a development of the Hail Mary.

4. A simple form of morning prayers.

5. A simple form of evening prayers.

Quotations

The children should learn these quotations in connection with the actual situation in which they were used. They should be frequently asked, Who said it? Where? When?

1. "God made heaven and earth."
2. "He hath given His angel charge over thee."
3. "Hail, full of grace! The Lord is with thee."
4. "Blessed art thou among women, and blessed is the fruit of thy womb."
5. "Glory to God in the highest and peace on earth to men of good will."
6. "Fear not, I bring you tidings of great joy."
7. "And falling down they adored Him."
8. "Now, O Lord, Thou dost dismiss Thy servant in peace."
9. "Take the Child and His mother and go into Egypt."
10. "He was subject to them."
11. "And not finding Him, they returned into Jerusalem seeking Him."
12. "He grew in age and wisdom and grace before God and men."
13. "And she shall bring forth a son: and thou shalt call His name Jesus. For He shall save His people from their sins" (Matt. i. 21).
14. "For, this day, is born to you a Savior, Who is Christ the Lord, in the city of David" (Luke ii. 11).

Hymns

Hymns are an important factor in reënforcing the general religious instruction and training, valuable for their own content, and, if properly taught, add an element of joy in religious instruction that is quite important. The child should, at the end of instruction, know the great hymns of the Church. For the first grade there is suggested the following to be sung within the voice range of the children.

1. Dear Angel
2. Beautiful Angel
3. Dear Little One

4. What Lovely Infant
5. Come Gather Here Children
6. Jesus, Teach Me How to Pray
7. Baby Jesus Smiling
8. Mother Mary
9. Mary, Mother of God
10. Why Do Bells for Christmas Ring?
11. Guardian Angel from Heaven so Bright

The Liturgy

The child should begin in the very first grade to be interested in the liturgy. But there is real danger of forcing his interest or loading him with information. A simple beginning could be made by having the child note the color of the vestments the priest wears at the Mass, and make them a basis for a first conception of the ecclesiastical year. Changes may be noted day by day and called to his attention.

Religious Practice

A definite part of the program in every grade is to build up the practice of religion in every grade and have the development cumulative throughout the grades. Wherever teachers see opportunity to build up Catholic practice they should do so. Teachers must not confound the lessons that may be essential and the actual practice in the life of the child. The pupil should understand the importance of interior disposition.

In the assignment to grades the purpose is to provide a specific time to see that the practice is established and understood. In some cases the habit will have been established. The cumulative listing of these practices is to emphasize the fact that they are not taught or established once and you are through with them. The practice must continue to be stimulated until it is "securely rooted in the life of the individual."

There should be emphasized in this grade: (1) morning prayer; (2) evening prayer; (3) regular attendance at Mass on Sundays; (4) attendance at Mass on all holydays of obligation.

Practical Life

The translation of the religious knowledge, practice, and attitudes in the day-to-day life of the child must always be an objective in religious education. The elevation of the actual daily life of the individual to a supernatural plane will come about through the character of the individual's motivation. This must be a matter of development: the child must be taken, however, where he is. The lines of development are indicated, but the more specific content is left for the experimentation of the first year.

1. Do a good turn every day for the love of God.
2. Cultivation of virtuous life.
3. Cultivation of school virtues.
4. Promotion of corporal and spiritual works of mercy.

References

1. Eaton, Mary, *The Little Ones*, B. Herder Co., 1922.

2. Brownson, Josephine Van Dyke, *To the Heart of the Child*.

3. Aurelia, Sister Mary and Kirsch, Rev. Felix M., *Practical Aids for Catholic Teachers* (Benziger).

4. Taggart, Marion Ames, *The Wonder Story* and *The Wonder Gifts*.

RELIGION IN GRADE I

INTRODUCTION

I. Manual for Grade I, Religion-in-Life Curriculum

This Teacher's Plan Book and Manual is a part of the Religion-in-Life curriculum. The text for Grade I is *The Book of the Holy Child*. In the Teacher's Manual each of the lessons in *The Book of the Holy Child* has been developed according to the following headings:

TO THE TEACHER
INTRODUCTION
PRESENTATION
DEVELOPMENTS
   Doctrine, Prayer, Hymns, Poems, Quotations, Virtuous Practices, Creative Music, Booklets, Dramatizations, Programs, Self-Expression, Creative Art, Picture Studies.
PICTURES
PUPIL'S READINGS
   All the stories listed under Pupil's Readings are taken from first-grade readers.
TEACHER'S REFERENCES
TEACHER'S NOTES

Texts

The text for religion in Grade I is *The Book of the Holy Child,* by Sister M. Bartholomew, O.S.F. (The Bruce Publishing Company, Milwaukee, Wisconsin.)

The work in Grade I during the first semester in religion is entirely oral; during the second semester the textbook is used. The book might be given as a Christmas present to the child by the parents.

First Semester

The work in religion for the first semester includes Parts I, II, III, and IV of the Teacher's Manual. The entire work of the semester is oral; no text is to be given to the children.

In every lesson the topics referring to *The Book of the Holy Child* and all the Pupil's Readings lists are to be used during the second semester only, when Parts I, II, III, and IV will be reviewed in connection with the lessons of the text.

Second Semester

The basic text for the second semester is *The Book of the Holy Child*. The work for the second semester covers a review of Parts I, II, III, and IV in connection with the lessons of the text, and the new Parts V and VI, and the Confession, Holy Mass, First Communion units.

II. Practical Suggestions for Teacher's Introduction to the Lesson

The Introduction to each lesson is merely a suggestion as to how the day's story may be approached. An effort has been made in the course to link up each lesson as closely as possible to that preceding, so that the child will have not only specific knowledge of the doctrine, but a general notion as to the meaning of the unit and of the year's work as well.

The Introductions have been varied, including the following suggestions: review questions, songs, poems, dramatizations, stories, oral and silent reading, socialized discussions.

Presentation

The teacher will frequently tell the story in its entirety. She will have the children grouped about her informally and tell them the story in an attractive and deeply religious manner. She will speak to them and permit them to ask a question about the story at any time.

The wording of the stories as given in the Presentations is

merely suggestive. It is understood that the teacher does not use the story verbatim, but rather that she adapt her language so far as possible to the comprehension of the children. When necessary she will explain the meaning of new or unusual words, according to any good method of learning new words and phrases.

At times the children should be grouped into smaller divisions and, with one elected as their chairman, should conduct their own class, telling the story to each other and asking each other questions about it. They should be encouraged frequently to tell the beautiful story to mother and father, or to read it to them and to the family at home, and to their friends.

Doctrine

In *The Book of the Holy Child*, the text for Grade I, all the necessary doctrine has been given the children in an interesting story form. The children are not to memorize the lessons, except at times some Scriptural texts or poems. Through a careful reading of the book, the child will incidentally learn the fundamental religious truths necessary for little children.

Warning!

Let the teacher be very conscientious and prudent in asking questions and explaining them, so as never, even for one instant, to place a doubt in the mind of the child regarding any doctrine of the Church. The following case serves as an example of a question capable of creating doubt:

Teacher: Was Jesus Christ truly God?

Pupil: Yes, Jesus Christ was truly God.

Teacher: *But* how could Jesus, *if He is God*, die on the Cross?

A statement like the above, *But* and *if He is God*, is indeed capable of making an exceedingly unfortunate and dangerous impression upon the mind of a little child.

Prayer

The prayers of the children should be few and simple. The Hail Mary is learned incidentally during the study of the Christmas lessons; likewise the first half of the Angelus. The oration to the Angelus should not be expected from children in the first grade. The Lord's Prayer will be studied during the second semester. Short morning, table, and evening prayers are to be taught. Short acts of Faith, Hope, Charity, Contrition are taught gradually in specific lessons of the course.

Every child should learn to say the ejaculatory prayers suggested in this course.

Hymns

The hymns suggested in the course should be taught during the regular daily singing class. Frequently the children should sing a hymn during the religion hour. At times they should be told to fold their hands because they are singing a prayer to God. They should always sing softly and with devotion. Occasionally a few of the children will sing the words while the others softly hum the melody. Suggest to them to sing these hymns softly in their hearts to Jesus when they visit Him in church; also to teach their little sisters and brothers the hymns they have learned in school.

Poems and Quotations

The teacher should have at her disposal a collection of suitable poems and quotations gathered from year to year for use in the religion classes. Some of the simpler poems could be memorized. Scriptural quotations must be explained to the children.

Some of the poems are intended for reading by the teacher to the class. This may be one method of introducing the day's lesson.

An exercise in drill in Scripture texts could be conducted as follows: The teacher will give the text and ask the class to tell under what situations and by whom it was first said. The children can test each other's knowledge of the texts in this same manner.

Points for Picture Study

Short, interesting sketch of the painter's life.

What the painter is particularly noted for in his pictures; e.g., Correggio, *light* and *music*.

The setting of the picture in the artist's life.

Artistic points about the picture which the teacher will bring out by good questions. Most important is to let the children tell what they like in the picture; why they like it; what story the picture tells them.[1]

The children may dramatize the pictures. It is of great interest and value for children to reproduce the various poses and actions in the picture. At times children may be arranged into groups, each group to represent one picture, while the other groups tell the story which the living picture represents. Simple costuming will add much to the effectiveness of this plan.

Appropriate music, songs, suggestive of the picture, may be sung while studying the picture or dramatizing it. With the study of the picture, *Holy Night*, the hymn, "Silent Night, Holy Night," should be sung.

The children should be encouraged to make their own picture book of the pictures studied during the religion hour.

Virtuous Practices

The hints for the practice of virtue in the child's life, which are referred to in the lessons, are usually a direct lesson learned from the story. It would be well at times to have the children suggest their own little practices.

Developments

Children must live their stories. The purpose of the developments is to give them the opportunity of really entering heart and soul into the beautiful life of Jesus. Every faculty of mind, heart, and soul of the child must be brought into play, must be exercised through a happy correlation of the work and play instincts.

Purposeful activities, in which, however, the child is permitted liberty of choice, will expand the powers of the soul and often cause the latent powers of mind to become active. The deep

---

[1]Rubber stamps of religious themes, e.g., Jesus in the Crib, Angels, with which to work out any of the stories in pictures and then to color these, may be had from the Creative Educational Society, Mankato, Minnesota.

emotional nature of the child will find ways and means of beautiful expression, if only the child be given his rightful opportunities. Teachers should not fear a loss of time, for how can that time be lost in which the pupil, through his creative art and expression, lives the beautiful stories of his little Leader, Jesus, in thought, word, and act?

As suggested again and again in the various units, the teacher need not take all the activities. Many have been noted; it is for her to select those appealing to her and most suitable to her class. She must always keep in mind the purpose of the activity, the coming close to Jesus in love by knowing Him better through every thought, word, and deed.

In these activities let the work often be carried out in a socialized manner. Have the class divided into small groups and seated or standing about informally, telling one another all about the story or about the project. The teacher can quietly pass from group to group and give her comments and commendations, or retell the story to the group. She must be the master hand guiding continually toward Christ.

Creative Song

Perhaps one phase of work which has been entirely neglected in the religion classes is that of creative music. Let the children compose their own songs and melodies, and sing them for the other classes. Children sing spontaneously, as can be well perceived when they are at play. Bring the creative song ability, inherent in almost every child, into play on many occasions. Praise every child for his attempt and tell him Jesus loves his very own song best of all.

Let the children suggest a title for a song that would be suitable for the lesson in question; e.g., at Christmas time the title, *Sweet Baby Jesus*.

Then talk over the rhythm, clap the rhythm, tap it, and sing it. Do this until the children are perfectly sure of the rhythm.

Now suggest that the class think of any words that will fit into this rhythm and follow the thought of the title. Let the children suggest one line at a time. Write these lines on the board, and let them choose which they like best. Continue until one stanza of four lines has finally evolved.

Now talk over what expression — soft, loud, tender — will best suit each line and each prominent word. Write this word above the line at the board.

Finally, let them quietly think of a melody of their own which will fit the first line. They will make their suggestions by singing their own melody. The teacher will write on the board in the musical syllables a few of the melodies suggested, and again let the children select which they like best. Continue in this way until the four lines have been completed.

(Adapted from "Creative Music," by Pearl Sanford, *The Instructor*, January, 1932.)

Booklets

Children always delight in making booklets. A number of booklets has been suggested in this course for Grade I. The teacher need not make them all, although they are arranged in such time order that all can be done. As a general rule these booklets should be simple, clean, and neat. The size depends upon the wish of the teacher and the class.

The main purpose of this activity is to impress more deeply upon the heart and mind of the child, the religious ideals to be inculcated by each one, particularly the one prevailing thought of the year: Jesus loves me.

Pictures, poems, original drawings, quotations, memory gems, and various other devices can be used in making the booklets. The children should be free to go on as they wish, while again the teacher guides and inspires to beautiful work for the love of Jesus.

Dramatization

The work in religion, Grade I, is very well adapted to dramatizations. The children should be given ample opportunity to express their creative abilities. Dramatization is among the principal methods of self-expression. The children should be allowed their own selection of words, but where the exact Biblical quotations are possible, they should be used.

Programs

The programs suggested in the course are to be very informal, a natural result of the day's feast, lesson, or some civic celebration. Some little touches in the way of clothes, headdress, furniture can be added to produce the required atmosphere.

The pastor, the Sister Superior, other classes, and parents should be invited occasionally. This will help to arouse and keep up the enthusiasm of the class. The teacher should be sure to keep in mind that all these programs are to be another means of lifting the child's heart to good and holy things. While not forcibly dragging in religion, the religious spirit naturally should pervade each program.

Self-Expression

In creative art, writing, song, and dramatization, a child can be given opportunities for the expression of his religious emotions. These opportunities should not be neglected. Indeed, if we wish a Catholic laity which will assert its rights, which will stand before the world ready to express its convictions, we must start early in the life of the child, giving him many opportunities for self-expression.

Pupil's Readings

It would be most advantageous to have as many supplementary first-grade readers in the classroom as possible. Certainly many Catholic readers, recognized by authorities as good, should be at hand continually and the children given free access to them. They will enjoy looking up their own stories, reading them, and finally telling them to the class. All these stories must refer to the unit in religion which is being studied at the time. In the lessons of the manual just a few readers have been noted; it is understood that many more excellent first-grade readers should be in the hands of the children.

Non-Catholic readers contain very fine character stories which might well fit into a unit in this religion course; e.g., stories of honesty, unselfishness, courtesy. The teacher ought to encourage the reading of these stories, also the retelling of the same in the religion or oral-English classes.

One corner of the room should be fitted out very simply for the library. A few small chairs and tables would help greatly in creating a reading atmosphere. The children may be given colored cards on which they can note in a simple way each time they have consulted another reader and have read a story in it.

Teacher's Notes

The space left for the teacher's notes should be well utilized. In it should be noted any improvements, criticisms, or other suggestions that might be helpful either for the teacher herself in coming years or for a revision of this plan. It should also contain information as to the sources of helpful material used, such as poems, texts, pictures, and activities that proved unusually successful. Pupil reactions and suggestions should also be noted. These should be sent at the end of the year to the publishers, The Bruce Publishing Company, to be used in future revisions of the textbooks and manuals.

General

Pupils should be encouraged again and again, after the first few weeks are over, to show the results of their efforts to their parents, to tell them their little stories, to read the stories in *The Book of the Holy Child* to them, to get them to pray with them, to go to Holy Communion or to Mass with them. Many a careless Catholic has been brought back to the Church through the innocent words of a child.

The lessons in religion should never be a thing apart. That does not mean that religion must be forcibly dragged into every activity of the day, but rather that the whole atmosphere in a Catholic school must be a religious one. In the study of the various units, the appearance of the classroom will help much to create this atmosphere.

After all is said and done, the teacher is and always must be a very important factor in the teaching of religion. The more she realizes her exalted position, the more conscientious she will be in preparing herself for the great work of leading the little ones ever closer to the Heart of the God-man, Jesus Christ.

Various Devices and Suggestions

1. *Game of Pictures:* A child steps before the class and says, "I see a picture," then proceeds to explain the figures on the picture he has in mind. The others will guess what the picture is and will retell the story it portrays.

2. *Game:* Children put their heads on the desk and think about a story. When Sister calls a name, the child will run to the front of the room and tell a few things about the story.

3. The children may draw a picture to go with each stanza of a poem they like.

4. Make a list of words suggested by any picture they study.

5. Write on the board phrases occurring in any lesson and let the class make pictures which they see in these words: e.g., the waves were wild, the stars were twinkling.

6. Have the children make a dictionary of words that have occurred in their lesson. They may call this: My Own Religion Word Book.

7. *Game:* What would you have done had you been a bird in Paradise? Let the children ask each other questions like this.

8. *Game:* Let the children make riddles: I was healed by Jesus when He was far away. Who am I? (The sick servant.) I was with Jesus in a boat. Who am I?

9. Copy all the words in the lesson that begin with a capital letter.

10. *Mental word pictures:* Tell what picture comes to your mind when I say: There was a terrible storm at sea.

11. *Classroom bulletin:* Pictures, sentences, words, drawings, announcements to the children, announcement to definite children what they may do.

12. Write the names of all the things you can see in the picture.

13. Coöperative posters in which every child of the class is working at one thing for the poster. Wrapping paper is very good for the background.

14. "Today is Johnnie's birthday, the day when God gave him to his dear parents. Have you wished him a happy birthday?" Birthday or name-day greetings to each child may be written on the board or pasted on the bulletin board.

15. *Game:* Let the children draw a star, fish, mountain, angel, shepherd, camel, crib, donkey, anything they wish, each on a separate sheet. They will hold up their drawing and ask the others what story they know from their religion class which tells them of a star, of a fish, etc.

UNIT I

CHRIST AND THE CHILDREN

Christ and the Little Children
September, 1st Week

Introduction:

Since all the work of the first grade is to be centered around Christ and the child, in the first few recitation periods the teacher must emphasize the truths that Jesus Christ is God, that Christ loves His child, that the child must love Christ, must be good because Jesus wants Him to be good.

Story:

"Once upon a time a tiny little Baby Boy came from heaven. That little Boy was God. His Mother called Him Jesus. Jesus was a little Child just like you, only He was God. Who can tell me something about Jesus?"

Let the children tell all they can about Jesus and recite any little prayers they may know. Some children will know nothing about God or Jesus. The teacher should take a special interest in these and often speak to them individually about Jesus.

At times the children can be arranged into groups, each consisting of a few well instructed and a few poorly instructed in religion. The better informed of the group can tell the others all they know about Jesus. The teacher will pass from group to group and give the necessary individual instruction.

Thus the foundations of socialized recitations can be laid in the first days of school life. The teacher should feel herself highly privileged to bring God's little ones ever closer to Him.

"The little Boy, Jesus, grew up to be a big, beautiful man. He was so good to all the people. He loved especially the little boys and girls like you."

12

Study the wall picture *Jesus Blessing Little Children.* Have the children speak freely about it and repeat the story again and again.

"Here is a picture of Jesus. See all the little children with Jesus. They loved Jesus because He was so good to them. What do you think the children on the picture are saying to Jesus? Which little child would you like to be? What would you say to Jesus if you could sit on His lap? Tell Jesus on the picture: 'Jesus, I love You. Make me a good little child.' "

Introduction:

Again show the picture, *Christ Blessing Little Children,* to the children on the next day. "In whose arms are the little children? Who is Jesus? Does Jesus love good little children very much? Tell Jesus again that you love Him."

If possible, give each child a picture of *Jesus Blessing Children,* and say to them:

"The picture is yours. Tell Jesus very softly, 'Jesus, I love You. Jesus, You are God.' Jesus loves you very much. He gave you to your good mother and father when you were a little baby. He takes care of you all the time. Say, 'Thank You' to Jesus. Pray to Jesus: 'Dear Jesus, bless my mother and father. Make me a good child. I love You, Jesus.' "

Story:

"One evening Jesus was very tired. He sat down to rest. Some mothers brought their little children to Jesus to bless them. Then some big men said, 'Go away, Jesus is too tired.' But Jesus said, 'Come, My little children, I want you. I love you.' And the little boys and girls ran to Jesus. He lifted them up in His arms. He put His hands on their little curly heads and blessed them. That is what Jesus is doing on your picture. Jesus blessed their sweet mothers, too. But it was getting dark and Jesus told the children they must go home. All the children said, 'Good night, Jesus. We shall come again. We love You.' They waved their hands to Jesus and went home, skipping and jumping, because Jesus had made them so happy.

"What did Jesus tell those little children? Would you like to visit Jesus, too? Who knows where Jesus lives? Jesus lives in a little golden house in church. We cannot see Him, but He is there. Tomorrow morning we shall go to visit Jesus. What will you say to Him? Jesus will be so happy when He sees you come to visit Him."

Often during the day as opportunities present themselves, point to the picture and say, "Jesus loves you, children. Whisper softly to Him, 'I love You, Jesus.' "

The teacher might at times turn to the picture and say, "Jesus, all the little boys and girls love You"; or, "Jesus, bless little Johnnie, little Mary" (naming the children of the class). During the first week each child's name ought to be mentioned. This can be done as a special reward for any act deserving commendation.

A Visit to Jesus
September, 2nd Week

Introduction:

The next morning's class should be a visit to Jesus in the Blessed Sacrament. Take the children as near to the Tabernacle as possible. Let them kneel and fold their hands.

Story:

"Children, here is Jesus' Home. Jesus is just behind this little door, looking and smiling at you. He loves you just as much as He loved the little children on the picture. Whisper to Jesus, 'Jesus, I love You. Bless my mother and father. Make me a good child.' "

When the children have returned to school, ask them such questions as: Who is Jesus? Where does Jesus live? What did you say to Jesus?

Now teach them how to conduct themselves in church. Just a few points ought to be mentioned; namely, never to talk in church, not to play but to look at Jesus in His golden house and keep on saying, "Jesus, I love You. Bless mother and father. Make me a good child."

Practice the genuflection. The children should be taught these first days to say at each genuflection: "Jesus, I adore You."

Teacher's References:[1]

The Little Ones, pages 103–105, "Suffer the Little Children."

Teacher's Notes:

The Sign of the Cross
September, 2nd Week

Introduction:

"Yesterday you went to visit Jesus in His little home on the altar. Jesus smiled at you and blessed you. You cannot see Him, but He is always there. He wants you to speak to Him. I am going to tell you a little prayer which Jesus wants you to say to Him."

Instruction:

Show the children the large wall crucifix. Let them touch it and say: "Jesus, loves me. I love Jesus." Tell them very briefly that Jesus died on the cross, because He loved them. Say nothing more about the Passion. Tell them Jesus will love them if they love His cross. They can make a cross on themselves like this:

The teacher makes the Sign of the Cross very slowly on herself, not saying any words. The children make it upon themselves while the teacher does so. Tell the children to make it very devoutly otherwise Jesus will not know it is His cross.

After the children know how to make the Sign of the Cross properly, teach them to use holy water with it. Start every class with the Sacred Sign.

---

[1]For full title, author, and publisher of any book mentioned under "Teacher's References" see Bibliography at the end of this book.

Let the children cut or tear a cross from paper and color it. They can mold one from clay, or trace one on the sand table. While they are engaged in this work, the teacher should repeat the words devoutly and let the children do the same.

Teacher's References:

The Little Ones, pages 11–14, "The Sign of the Cross."

Teacher Tells a Story, "The Cross on the Locket."

Leading the Little Ones to Christ, page 9, "Sign of the Cross."

Teacher's Notes:

UNIT II

THE CREATION

God the Creator of Heaven
God Made the Angels
September, 2nd Week; February, 1st Week

To the Teacher:

Wherever there is a direction to use the text, *The Book of the Holy Child,* it is to be followed in the second semester only, since there will be no book in the hands of the children during the first semester. All the children's references for reading are for the second semester only.

Introduction:

"Once upon a time there lived a great, good, holy King. He could do anything He wanted to. There was nothing at all that this King could not make. He needed only to wish for something, and there it was.

"Dear children, this great, good, holy King is God! He made the big, beautiful heaven for His very own home. He made each one of you, too, to be His own dear little child, to live with Him in heaven some day."

Presentation:

"A long time ago God lived all alone in His grand heaven. He wanted to make others happy with Him in His palace, heaven. But there was nobody living. God had not yet made anyone. Remember, there is nothing that God cannot do. God just had to think: 'I want many lovely angels with Me in heaven.' And, children, all at once millions and millions and millions of the most glorious angels were made! They adored their great God and King. They filled His heavens with the sweetest songs: 'Holy,

Holy, Holy!' God loved His angels and gave them His beautiful heaven for their home. The angels could not be happier. They were most beautiful, wise, and holy. They were with God."

"Can you find the first picture in your new book? What do you think Jesus is saying? Why are His arms stretched out? Why do you like the picture? This same Jesus made the beautiful angels. Look at the next picture in your book." Let them talk much about the picture. "Now let us read our very first lesson. Who will try?"

Show the children as many beautiful angel pictures as possible. Study with them the angels in the picture, *Christmas Chimes.* Let them tell each other and the teacher, too, what they can about the picture.

Have the children repeat the story frequently of the creation of the angels.

The Fall of the Angels

Introduction:

Review Questions: Who made heaven? Whom did God make to live in heaven with Him? How did God make the angels? What did the angels do when God had made them? Would you like to live in heaven with God and the angels?

Presentation:

"God had made those lovely angels for Himself. God was their loving Father. He was so good to them. He gave them His beautiful home. The angels had to obey God, because God was their Father. Children, the angels were so grand, and glorious, and wise, and powerful. Soon some of them became very proud. They thought they were like God. Lucifer, the brightest of the angels, and the other proud angels, disobeyed their good God. That was very, very bad. Michael and all the other good angels obeyed God. The good angels fought against the bad angels. God threw Lucifer, that wonderful angel, into hell; and all the other bad angels, too. And they were all changed into the most awful, horrid, mean devils."

Study the picture, *St. Michael and the Dragon,* by Raphael.

"Lucifer and the other bad angels will never, never again be beautiful; they will never again be in heaven with God. But the good angels are still in God's home, happy and holy."

Stress the points that Lucifer and the bad angels made themselves unhappy by their disobedience to God; that God is all pure and holy and good; that He had to punish them because they were so bad.

A set of angel pictures by Fra Angelico could be mounted and placed before the children for enjoyment. It is true the children will not understand them entirely, but surrounding them from early youth with the beautiful will no doubt have a lasting effect for the good.

Teacher's References:

To the Heart of the Child, Lesson III, "The Angels."

The Little Ones, pages 16–25, "The Angels."

Leading the Little Ones to Christ, pages 38–41, "Our Return of Love: Obedience."

The Catholic School Journal, September, 1931, "The Angels."

Teacher's Notes:

God the Creator of the World

To the Teacher:

Throughout the study of this unit, artistically colored pictures of nature, of plants and animals should be placed in the classroom in view of the children. As the stories of the creation develop from day to day, the teacher will call attention in these pictures to the specific phase of creation under discussion.

The children might bring their picture books from home, show them to their companions in class while pointing out the objects in the light of this truth: God is the Creator of all things; He made all for us.

After Christmas, when *The Book of the Holy Child* is to be used as the text, the stories of creation will be reviewed through the lessons of this unit in correlation with the lessons in the text on pages 2, 3, 4, 5, and 6.

The words of the text are the doctrinal statements of the truths of religion involved in this unit. The pictures mentioned above as also those of the text will aid both pupil and teacher in this review. There is no formal memorization of any lesson. The children will have mastered the truths incidentally as the lessons are frequently reviewed.

God Made the Light
September, 3rd Week; February, 1st Week
Introduction and Presentation:

"A long, long time ago God and His angels alone were living. In the beginning God made heaven and earth. There were no little boys or girls, no mothers or fathers, no flowers or birds. No sun, no moon, no stars lighted the heavens. It was all dark, dark. God wanted His earth, and, children, there it was! God just needs to think what He wants. Now God said in this darkness: 'Let there be light!' Suddenly light was made, and the earth was covered with it. God called this light day, and the darkness He called night. God made the earth, the light, the darkness for you. He made the light for you, because He loved you, His child. He made the night for you, too. Who can tell me why God made the night?"

Have the children talk about the story and ask questions about it. Get them to understand gradually that in the beginning there was nothing but God. God always was and always will be. He alone had no beginning. Let them repeat softly again and again: "God made the light for me. Thank You, dear God. I love You."

Let the children make a Creation Booklet. This activity runs parallel with the study of the unit.

Darkness and Light: A piece of black construction paper on which the teacher has traced a circle, is given to the child. He cuts out the circle. A circle the same size as the black one, has been traced by the teacher on white drawing paper. This is also cut by the child. While the children are cutting out these circles, the teacher repeats the story of the creation of light. (If the child is unable to handle the scissors, the teacher will have these circles ready to give to him.) The children could say quietly while at work: "God made the light for me."

Let the children point out different objects in Nature or on the pictures while saying: "In the beginning there were no trees, no houses, no little boys and girls, no light."

It is important that the children be given ample opportunity to express themselves freely about the lessons they are learning.

God Made the Sky
September, 3rd Week; February, 1st Week

Introduction:

A short review of the preceding lesson through the following questions: What happened when God said: "Let there be light"? How did God make the light? What did He call the light? What did He call the darkness? For whom did God make the light? What should you say to God because He made the Day and the Night for you?

Presentation:

"God wanted to make many other beautiful things for you. He loved you, His little child, so much. On the first day God made the light for all of us. The next day He said: 'Let there be a blue sky!' At once the big, beautiful sky covered the earth. God loved this sky and He called it the heavens."

Sky Booklet: Each child has his white circle. With blue chalk or crayon, he colors half of it to represent the blue sky. This part of the story of creation is repeated by the teacher and the pupils as the children are working.

"Only God could make the big, beautiful sky, and He made it for you, and me, and all of us. We must love God very much because He is so good to us. You must love God very, very much because He is so good to you. Look up, way into the sky and say very softly to God: 'Thank You, God, for Your beautiful sky. I love You.' "

God Made the Land and the Sea
September, 4th Week; February, 1st Week

Introduction:

A short review of the preceding lessons should be given as follows: Who made the beautiful, blue sky? What else did God make? How did God make the light and the sky? For whom did God make the light and the sky? God loved you very much to make them for you. You, too, must love Him very, very much and thank Him often.

Teach the following either as a poem or as a song:

THE CREATION[1]

All things bright and beautiful,
All things great and small,
All things wise and wonderful,
The Lord God made them all.

Presentation:

"On the first day God made the light, and on the second day He made the blue sky. The earth was all covered with deep water." Study the picture in the text on page 2, or any other representative of the story. "Then on the third day God said:

" 'Let the waters be gathered together into one place, and let the dry land appear.' At once the water rolled away into oceans, lakes, and rivers. And there was the dry land, just as God wanted it.

"God then made the trees, and the lovely plants and flowers

---

[1]From *The Sunday Book of Poetry*, by Cecil Alexander. By permission of The Macmillan Company, publishers. Music for this poem will be found in *The Child's Song Treasury*, by Mary B. Ehrmann.

to grow on this dry land." Study the pictures in the text, pages 3 and 4. "He did this all for you. He thought of His little child and wanted to make the earth most beautiful for you. What should you tell God when you see the pretty trees and flowers?"

Land-and-Sea Booklet: The children color the other half of the circle, a part of it brown to represent land, and the other part blue-green to represent sea. Repeat the story and such statements as: God made the sea. God made the land.

Paste small pictures of flowers and trees on the land. Say, "God made the flowers for me. God loves me. I thank You, dear God."

Arrange the sand table from day to day as the story of creation develops. The children should be very active in the working out of this project. They might bring their little toy birds and animals from home. The story of creation is retold as the sand table is arranged. Such statements as "God loves me. God made all things," should be repeated often. Make the sand table as beautiful as possible.

The pictures should be in constant view of the children. A short picture study could be a part of the oral-expression class. Let the children hold the pictures and tell what they know about them and about creation.

Simple health and safety rules, of fresh air and water, could be advantageously taught in connection with the lessons on, God made the sky, the land, and the sea. Develop the idea that they must take care of their bodies and keep them clean; God wants it so, because their beautiful souls live in their bodies. Let the children join in the talk as much as possible.

Children plant flower seeds in window boxes and care for them. Keep before their minds that God has made the seeds to grow and to produce flowers for them.

The children's attention should be directed to the beauty of flowers and leaves. Bouquets of the same could be placed in the classroom. Again the thought that God made them so beautiful should raise the mind and heart of the child from Nature to Nature's God. The teacher can do this by a few simple, appropriate statements.

God Made the Sun, Moon, and Stars
September, 4th Week; February, 1st Week

Introduction:

"Who can show on the pictures what God made on the second day? Who can show the class what God made on the third day? For whom did God make all these beautiful things? God must have loved you very much to make all this for you."

Let the children repeat such simple sentences as the following, while they point to the pictures: "God made the blue sky. God made the lovely flowers. God made the trees. God made these for me. God loves me, His little child. I love God, too. Thank You, dear God."

Presentation:

"On the fourth day God made a beautiful big light to shine and keep us warm during the day. God wanted this light to make the flowers and trees grow, and to make His little children happy. He made other lights to shine for us at night. Can you tell me what light God made for the day? What light did He make to shine during the night? How did God make them? What did God say when He wanted to make something? Remember only God can make such wonderful things. God made the sun, the moon, and the stars just for you. When your father gives you something, what should you say? A polite child always says, 'Thank you,' when someone is kind to him. But God has been the kindest to you. You must not forget to be polite to God and often say, 'Thank You,' to Him."

Booklet on Sun, Moon, Stars: The teacher will have small circular pieces of yellow and silver paper ready to give to the children. Gold and silver stars can be purchased for ten cents a box, one hundred in a box (Dennison's). While the children are pasting these in their circles, this part of the story of creation is reviewed.

God Made the Animals
September, 4th Week; February, 1st Week

Introduction:

A Short Review: "What did God make on the fourth day? What did He make on the other days? Show on the pictures what God made each day, and say: 'God made the stars. God made the sun. God made the flowers. God made everything for me.'"

Teach the second stanza of *The Creation*, by Cecil Alexander:[2]

Each little flower that opens,
Each little bird that sings,
He made their glowing colors,
He made their tiny wings.

Study the pictures again on pages 4 and 5.

Presentation:

"God loved everything that He had made, the flowers, the trees, the lakes. The stars were in the sky, the trees and flowers were on the earth. God wanted something beautiful to fly in the sky; something to swim and play in the waters; and something to run and crawl on the earth. Now, when the fifth day came, God made all kinds of fishes to swim and play in the water. He made many beautiful birds to fly and sing in the sky. He made many animals to live on the earth. God made them all for you because He loved His little child so much."

Animal Booklet: Very small pictures of fish, birds, animals will be pasted by the children in their respective places on the circle. Again the story is repeated.

Instead of individual booklets, one large class chart could be made by the children under the direction of the teacher.

Discuss with the children the different animals, birds, fishes, they know. Let them talk freely about their pet animals. Incidentally these lessons on creation can be made an interesting and de-

[2]From *The Sunday Book of Poetry*, by Cecil Alexander. By permission of The Macmillan Company, publishers.

lightful nature study, always directing the child's mind to the Creator.

Make a short story of the life of a bird the children know, its song, its beauty, its usefulness. Tell the children that God cares for the birds and the flowers; that He loves children much more than these and that He protects and cares for them.

The love and goodness of God, His care for His creatures, and His power over all created things must be kept before the minds of the children in such a way as to instill in them a great love for Him and implicit trust in His tender care.

Have a goldfish aquarium in the classroom. Stock it with a few fish, a small turtle, and snails. The beautiful lessons and the joy derived by the children from ·watching these will amply repay the small care they need. Ask the children: Who made the fish so beautiful? Why did God make these things? and similar questions.

Have a short discussion on kindness to animals. Let the children suggest how they can be kind to them. Repeat that God made the animals and that He wants us to be kind to them.

Take a walk through the woods, through a park, to the lake, for the purpose of seeing God's creation and becoming more observant. Continually call attention to God as the Creator of all this beauty for His child.

Other Activities: Review the story of creation from day to day. All the activities must be directed toward the lesson of the week. The teacher may select any of the activities or supply those she herself has devised. A few additional activities are offered:

Dramatization: Let the children imagine they are the flowers, birds, rabbits, or anything else in Paradise. They will tell how God created them and what they know about the creature they are impersonating. Here is an excellent opportunity for creative work and play.

Clay modeling: Let the children model anything they wish in connection with creation. Even though the work is not perfect, the teacher should appreciate and encourage them in their self-expression.

Read and discuss the following poem:

THE CREATION

In heaven, up above
Dwells the Father, God of love,
He made the earth; He made the sky,
The ocean wide, the mountains high,
He made each flower and bird and tree,
He made you, and He made me.
He sends the snow; He sends the rain;
He makes the flowers bloom again;
And when the earth is bleak and bare;
He feeds the birdies everywhere.

                                        — *Berdice Moran*

Teach the following as a song, if music is available: *The Creation,* by Cecil F. Alexander.

End this lesson with a reading of all the lessons, pages 1 to 5, inclusive.

God Made Man
September, 4th Week; February, 2nd Week

Introduction:

"When God had made the sun and moon and stars and all the animals and plants, the earth was a beautiful place on which to live. It was like a lovely park with large trees, bright flowers, and sparkling water. Was there anything left for God to make after that?" Let the children make suggestions.

Presentation:

"When the earth was ready, God made the most beautiful of all things. The Lord God took the slime of the earth and made a body of it. But the body could not move; it had no life. Then the Almighty God breathed into the beautiful face of this body. At once the body became a living man, because God had breathed a soul into it. This was the first man on earth. His name was Adam."

Let the children repeat again and again the story of Adam's

creation. Stress the fact of the soul's beauty; the soul gives the body life; the soul makes us think and pray.

Review the Sign of the Cross.

Teacher's References:

The Little Ones, M. Eaton, "God Made Everything," pages 14, 15, 53, 54.

To the Heart of the Child, Brownson, Lesson I, "God the First Cause."

Practical Aids for Catholic Teachers, Sister M. Aurelia, Rev. F. M. Kirsch, "Thankfulness," page 33; "God's Creatures Serve Us," page 34; "Kindness to Animals," pages 27–32; "Dramatization," pages 234–238.

Teacher Tells a Story, Rev. Jerome Hannan. "Creation," Vol. I, pages 52–68.

A Child's Garden of Religion Stories, Rev. P. H. Matimore, "How God Made the World," Chapter I; "The Garden of Paradise," Chapter II.

Art Education Through Religion, "Animals," Vol. I, page 25; "Clay Modeling," page 25.

Leading the Little Ones to Christ, "God the Creator of All Things," pages 23 to 38.

Teacher's Notes:

Adam and Eve
October, 1st Week; February, 2nd Week

Introduction:

Review as follows: "Who can tell me how God made the world? the birds? the flowers? What did God make last of all?

How did God make Adam? What did God breathe into Adam's body? Yes, He gave him a soul that will never die. The soul made Adam the most beautiful of all things that God had created. It made him think and speak and act. It made him the image of God. God loved Adam more than all His other creatures. Why do you think God loved him more?"

Presentation:

"When God saw Adam standing before Him, tall, strong, beautiful, and good, He was happy. He took Adam into a wonderful garden called Paradise."

As the stories are reviewed, the following activities can be used to vitalize them. Not all these need be taken. The teacher will select those that appeal to her or use others of her own choice.

Finish the sand-table project, the Garden of Paradise. Make the Garden as beautiful as possible with grass, flowers, trees, lake, stream, birds, animals. The Tree of Knowledge, with fruit cut from colored paper, and the serpent on it, should be most conspicuous.

" 'All this is yours,' God said. 'I made everything for you.' Then He brought all the birds and animals to Adam. Adam gave them a name."

Dramatization: One of the children, representing Adam, takes his position in the front of the room. The others pass by him and he gives each of them the name of a bird and other animal. As the child leaves "Adam" he imitates in some suitable way, the animal whose name he has received. He might also tell all he knows about that creature. God, the Master of all things, and man as His steward, must be the lesson to be inculcated.

"Adam was happy in the Garden of Paradise. It was the loveliest garden on the whole earth. The animals came right up to him and never did any harm. Beautiful flowers grew all around him. The birds sang their sweetest songs and many of the trees had fruit which Adam could eat. God said to Adam: 'You may eat fruit of every tree in the garden except from the one which I shall show you. If you eat of that tree you shall die.' Adam loved God. He wanted to do everything that God told him. He was very happy. But he had no one to be happy with him. He was all alone in Paradise. God said: 'It is not good for man to be alone.' Then God did another most wonderful thing. He put Adam into a deep sleep. And when Adam was asleep, God took one of the bones from his side and made a beautiful woman with it. When Adam awoke from his deep sleep, God brought this woman to him and gave her to Adam." Study the picture in the text, page 6. "Adam was very happy. The name of this first woman was Eve."

Adam and Eve Disobey God

Introduction:

Have the children tell all they can about Paradise. Let them talk freely and use pictures to help along whenever possible.

"Was Adam happy in Paradise? How did he get something to eat? Could he take fruit from all the trees in Paradise? What did God tell him? Whom did God give to Adam? How did God make Eve? Tell how Adam and Eve were made by God."

Presentation:

"Adam and Eve were very happy in Paradise." Now read the lesson on page 6, and again study the picture.

Duologue between Adam and Eve about the birds, the trees, the flowers, and about the Tree of Knowledge.

ADAM (wandering about the garden, sees a beautiful flower; he calls): Eve, Eve, come quickly. See the pretty flower growing on this bush.

EVE (comes and looks at the flower): Oh, Adam, how good God is to us. What shall we call it?

ADAM: Let us call it Rose.

EVE: Rose, Rose, what a pretty name. Let us thank God for making the rose for us. (They kneel down and thank God.)

Let the children continue this duologue for some time.

"Adam told Eve what God had said about the fruit tree from which they did not dare to eat. Eve also wanted to obey God. She did not want to eat the fruit of that tree. But one day as she was walking in the Garden of Paradise, she came to this tree.

The fruit was beautiful, and large, and ripe. On this tree was a serpent. It was really the devil who had hidden himself inside of the serpent. The devil hates God. He tries to get people, little boys and girls, too, to do wrong. He did not like to see Adam and Eve so happy. He said to Eve: 'Why does God not let you eat the fruit of this tree?' Eve answered: 'If we eat of this fruit, we will die.' 'That is not true,' said the serpent. 'If you eat from this tree, you will be very wise.'

"Do you think Eve should have stopped to listen to the serpent? What should you do if one of your little friends tells you to do something bad? (Talk a little while on good companionship.) Eve should have gone away, because she knew it was wrong for her to eat that fruit. She knew God loved her and Adam very much. She knew she should obey the good God who had made them so happy. But Eve listened to the serpent. Instead of running away, she began to look at the lovely fruit on the tree. By and by she wanted some of it. She put up her hand and picked some. She ate it. Then she called Adam and gave him some. Adam, too, disobeyed God and ate of the forbidden fruit. Oh, how very sad they became."

Study pictures on pages 6 and 7. Note the contrast of color in the two pictures.

Speak to the children on obedience toward their parents who take God's place; also on asking their parent's permission when they want something; not to steal anything at all.

"Now we shall read the story in our own books on pages 5, 6, and 7. Who will read the first line? Who else would like to read?" Have the children read the lesson on page 5.

"Read the part you like best on page 6. Find the line on page 5 which tells you why God made all things. What did God say to Adam and Eve after they had not obeyed Him? You will find this on page 7."

End the lesson with a hymn to Jesus.

Punishment of Adam and Eve
October, 2nd Week; February, 1st Week

Introduction:

The teacher recites or reads slowly, beautifully, the following poem by Marion Dixon Thayer:

EXCUSES[3]

O God, why am I ever bad
When I know that it makes You sad?
And oh, why don't I always do
The things that You have told me to?
Dear God, dear God, I'm very small —
But that is no excuse at all.

"Were Adam and Eve always good in Paradise? What did they do? Why did Eve take the forbidden fruit? Who was the serpent? Why did the serpent want Eve to take the forbidden fruit? What should Eve have done when the serpent told her not to obey God?"

Presentation:

"As soon as Adam and Eve had eaten of the forbidden fruit, they knew they had done wrong. They were very much afraid because they had disobeyed God. They were sorry and ashamed because God loved them so much and had been so good to them. They were no longer happy. They were afraid of God, their good Father in heaven."

Read the lesson on page 7 again.

"God sent them out of the beautiful garden. They had to work and suffer much. After many years of sorrow, they had to die. They could not go to heaven, because God had closed heaven to them when they disobeyed Him. God pitied them. He promised that some day He would send His own Son, Jesus, to save them and to open the gates of heaven again. See how good God is. He loves His naughty children, if they tell Him they are sorry."

---

[3]From *The Child on His Knees* (page 117), by Marion Dixon Thayer. By permission of The Macmillan Company, publishers.

Show Doré's picture, *Adam and Eve Driven Out of Paradise.* Let the children repeat the story and talk about the picture.

Show Munier's *The Christ Child.* Tell the children that Jesus is the Son of God, the One whom God promised to Adam and Eve in Paradise. Show a picture of Mary, explaining that she was to be the Mother of Jesus, the Promised One.

Rearrange the sand table to represent the story of Adam and Eve driven from Paradise. Let one half of it still be very beautiful; on the other half show the barrenness of the earth. Place an angel with a sword at an entrance into Paradise. A wall might be placed around Paradise, with a gate to illustrate the entrance.

Tell the children, when they have been naughty, to say to God: "Dear God, I am sorry I have made You sad. I won't do it again." Encourage them to tell their parents when they have done something naughty; also to ask mother and father to forgive them.

Teacher's References:

The Holy Bible, Genesis, Chapters I, II, and III.

Leading the Little Ones to Christ, "God's Goodness to Us," pages 30–33; "God is Everywhere," pages 49–59.

The Little Ones, "Adam and Eve," pages 59–61.

To the Heart of the Child, "Adam and Eve," Lessons IV and V.

The Child's Garden of Religion Stories, Matimore, "The Garden of Paradise," pages 9–19.

Practical Aids, "God's Omnipresence," page 40; sand-table work — equipment; sand, trees, grass, water, roads, mountains; "How to Work Out a Project," pages 227–230.

Teacher's Notes:

God Made Me
October, 3rd Week; February, 2nd Week

Introduction:

Study the picture in the text. Tell the class of the many children just like themselves on the whole earth; that God made them all; that God loves them; that they are their little sisters and brothers; that God wants them all to come to Him in heaven.

Let the children repeat the story of Adam and Eve, using the pictures of the preceding lessons.

Presentation:

"God made Adam and Eve. He wanted them to be happy in Paradise. They disobeyed Him. God loved Adam and Eve, but He had to punish them. He sent them out of the beautiful Paradise and they had to work very hard. They were sad and had much pain and sorrow. God felt sorry for them and He promised to send His own Son Jesus from heaven sometime to open the gates of heaven again.

"God did not leave Adam and Eve all alone. Soon He sent them many children. God made all the children. God makes all the children in the world. He is their good Father in heaven. He loves His little children. He wants all His children to come to Him some day in heaven. God made your mother and father. And, children, one day not so very long ago, the dear God made you, too. He gave you to your mother and father to take care of you, because He loved you so much. God is your Father in heaven. He made you for heaven. God made your eyes, your ears, your mouth, your whole body. God gave you a soul, as He gave one to Adam and Eve. You cannot see your soul, but it makes you think, and see, and feel, and do all that you can do. God made your soul so you could love Him. Your soul is God's own home. He is in your soul now. Whisper very softly to God: 'Dear God, I love You. Thank You for making me.' "

Have children read the lessons, "God is Our Father," "Robert's Prayer," "Heaven" in *The Book of the Holy Child,* pages 8 to 10, and study the accompanying pictures.

Heaven

Introduction:

Teacher recites or reads the poem, "The Baby," by George Macdonald.

Presentation:

"When God made you a little tiny baby, He gave you to your dear mother and father. He told them to take good care of you, His little child, because you are God's child. He wants you to live a little while on earth and then to be with Him in heaven always. You can go to heaven only if you have always been good. God gave you such good parents to help you to be good. You must often thank God for your kind mother and father and do whatever they tell you to do. Then God will love you and take you to heaven with all His beautiful angels."

Study the picture, *The Heavenly Messenger*, Kaulbach.

The teacher will now speak of heaven as a most beautiful place where all the good will live forever. She should make heaven as beautiful as she can picture it. (See the Apocalypse, Chapter IV, 21.) She shall speak of God whom we shall see in heaven, God who made us, who loves us; of some of the saints; of the angels. She will also tell the children of the natural joys in heaven, of seeing their parents, teachers, friends forever.

Let the children fold as a booklet a small sheet of drawing paper and paste pictures of a man and a woman, boy, girl, baby, in it. All these the teacher can get from catalogs. While the children are pasting them into the booklet, they can say quietly, "God made mother. God made baby. God made me. God made us for heaven." Pictures of Negro, Indian, Chinese children could be used and the thought of Christian brotherhood briefly developed.

Oral-Expression Class: The children tell about their mother, father, sisters, brothers, and about the baby. Teacher will continually stress the thought that God made them all, they belong to Him, He wants them all in heaven sometime.

"God made you, children, because He wanted you to come to Him in heaven. He gave you to your dear father and mother when you were a little baby, to help you on your way to heaven.

God loved you so much that He sent a most beautiful angel from heaven to help mother and father take care of you. He is your guardian angel. He is with you now; he is with you all the time. During the day your guardian angel sees and hears all you do and say. He is happy when his little child is good. And oh! he is so sad when you are naughty. Whisper to your beautiful, good angel now: 'My dear angel, help me to be good. Show me the way to heaven.' Your guardian angel always sees God and he always sees you! At night time your angel hears you say your night prayers. He stays with you all the night and prays for you. How kind your angel is to you. He wants to lead you all your life and when you die, your beautiful guardian angel will take you to God!"

Pictures to Be Studied:

To God — Kaulbach.

Christ and the Children — Plockhorst.

St. Mary, the Virgin — Ittenbach.

The Christ Child — Ittenbach.

Samuel at Prayer — Reynolds.

Baby Stuart — Van Dyck.

Read the lesson on page 10, "Heaven," once more.

The teacher reads the third stanza of *The Creation*[4] in a beautiful way. Let the children speak about the poem.

> He gave us eyes to see them,
>   And tongues that we might tell
> How great is God Almighty
>   Who has made all things well.

Review of Unit II

Appoint ten children to read before the entire class one lesson in the text up to page 10.

Let others describe the pictures in the text.

End the review lesson with a song to Jesus, to the Guardian Angel.

---

[4] From *The Sunday Book of Poetry*, by Cecil Alexander. By permission of The Macmillan Company, publishers.

UNIT III

MY BEST FRIENDS

Jesus
October, 4th Week; February, 3rd Week

Introduction:

"A long, long time ago the dearest, holiest little Boy lived on this earth. He came down from heaven. His name was Jesus. This little Boy is the great God, who made heaven and earth and all things for you. He made you."

Study the picture on page 11. Tell the children that Jesus is looking at each one and blessing him. Let them say softly to Jesus: "Jesus, I love You. Bless me."

Also show the children any beautiful art pictures of Jesus; e.g., *The Holy Child,* by Ittenbach and Munier.

Presentation:

"Jesus came down from heaven to live on earth because He loves you. He made you. He gave you to your parents. He blesses you. Some day He will take you to His beautiful heaven because He loves you. Jesus loves all good little boys and girls. Whisper to Jesus: 'I love You, too, dear Jesus.' "

In *The Book of the Holy Child,* read the lesson on page 11, "Jesus."

Tell the children that they can show their love for Jesus by being good, by saying their prayers, by obeying their parents, by being kind to the other children. Let them suggest a specific act which they will perform during this day.

Teach them to bow their heads slightly at the name of Jesus. End the lesson with a hymn to Jesus.

Mary
October, 4th Week; February, 3rd Week

Introduction:

"God sent Jesus from heaven as a tiny little Baby. He was just like every other little baby, just like the baby at your house. God gave Him a good, sweet mother. Her name was Mary. She is also called the Blessed Virgin. God gave you to a sweet mother, too, when you were little. What did Mother Mary do for Jesus?"

Let the children talk about all that Mary did for Jesus; about what their own mothers do for them.

Presentation:

"Jesus loved His holy Mother. She was so good to Him. Jesus wants you to love Mary, too. Mary is your mother in heaven. She sees you, she prays for you to God; she loves you. She wants you to come to heaven some day. Whisper to Mother Mary, 'Oh, Mary, I love you and Jesus.' "

Study the picture, *Mary*, in *The Book of the Holy Child*, page 12, and read the Lesson. Also study an art picture of Mary; e.g., *The Virgin Mary*, Ittenbach; *Mary*, Sister M. Stanisia.

Repeat the Hail Mary very devoutly and sing a hymn to Mary with devotion.

Joseph
October, 4th Week; February, 3rd Week

Introduction:

"Jesus and Mary needed someone to take care of them. God told a holy man, St. Joseph, to love Jesus and Mary and to work for them. Oh, how happy St. Joseph was to take care of the Son of God, Jesus, and Mary, the Blessed Virgin."

Study the picture of St. Joseph in *The Book of the Holy Child*, page 13, or any other picture of St. Joseph.

Presentation:

"St. Joseph loved Jesus and Mary more than anyone else on earth. He worked so hard for them. He was a carpenter. He built houses, and made chairs and tables and many other things for people. He built a house for Jesus and Mary and made all the furniture in it. Jesus and Mary loved St. Joseph and often thanked him for working for them. St. Joseph loved Jesus and Mary. He loves you also. He wants you to come to heaven some day. He often prays for you in heaven. Say to St. Joseph: 'St. Joseph, pray for me. I love you.' "

Read the lesson, "St. Joseph," in *The Book of the Holy Child*, page 13, and study the accompanying picture.

The Holy Family
October, 4th Week; February, 3rd Week

Introduction:

"Jesus, Mary, and Joseph are called the Holy Family. Because St. Joseph worked for Jesus and took care of Him, he is called the foster father of Jesus. Jesus' real Father is God the Father in heaven. The Blessed Virgin Mary was the sweet Mother of the Holy Family. She was the Mother of Jesus. Jesus was the Child of the Holy Family."

Presentation:

Have the children study the picture on page 14 or any other Holy Family picture and tell all they can about it. Ask who each member of the Holy Family is and what each did on earth.

Speak about the children's own family. Again let them tell all they want to. Tell them that God loves their family, too, as He loved the Holy Family.

"Now the Holy Family is in God's beautiful heaven. Mary and Joseph are happy with Jesus. From heaven they see you and often pray for you and for your dear ones at home. Say often to them: 'Holy Mary and St. Joseph, pray for me. Ask Jesus to bless our family.' "

Read the Lesson, "The Holy Family," page 14. Memorize the last sentence of the reading lesson, page 12, as a prayer.

Now study the picture, *At Prayer*, page 16, *The Book of the Holy Child*. The little children are praying to Jesus, Mary, and Joseph. They are asking the Holy Family in heaven to bless their mothers and fathers and dear ones. Good children ask God daily to bless their parents.

My Angel
October, 4th Week; February, 4th Week

Introduction:

Review questions: Who are some of your dear friends in heaven? What do they do for you? What must you be if you want to go to heaven sometime? Who remembers how God made His angels? What do the angels do in heaven?

Teach the children a hymn to the guardian angel, "Dear Angel" or "Beautiful Angel."

Presentation:

"God has loved you, His little child, so much. He wants you to come to heaven some day, and to stay with Him always. When the good God made you a few years ago, He gave you one of His very wonderful angels to help you on the way to heaven. He is your guardian angel. He takes care of you and loves you."

Study the picture, *The Guardian Angel*, by Guercino. Let the children discuss it in their infant ways with each other and with the teacher. Study the picture in *The Book of the Holy Child*, page 17, and read the lesson.

"He hath given His angels charge over thee (Matt. iv. 6). Ever since you were born, your guardian angel has been with you. He loves you because you are God's dear child. You can show your love for your good angel by often thinking of him. Every good child will think of his angel upon waking in the morning from sleep and just before going to sleep at night."

Teach the children the prayer "Beautiful Angel," *The Book of the Holy Child*, page 18. Say this prayer at times with the regular school prayer.

"All day long your angel sees you and hears you. When you are good, he is so happy. When you are naughty, he is sad because you have offended God."

Tell the story of St. Frances of Rome and her guardian angel; her feast is celebrated on March 9.

"Whenever you feel like doing something wrong, pray to your angel to help you. He will always help you to be good."

Have the children read and discuss the poem, "Oh! My Good Angel," *The Book of the Holy Child,* page 18.

"Children, your guardian angel will stay with you all through life. One day when you will have to die, he will still be with you. If you have been good and holy, he will take you to God. Then you and your good guardian angel will be together forever and forever with God in heaven."

Study Kaulbach's *Angel of Peace* or *To God.* Have the children repeat the various duties of their guardian angels.

"All the other children have a guardian angel like yours, too. Mother and father, little brother and sister, all have one to help them on the way to heaven. Tell your little brother tonight about his guardian angel. Our angels always see us, and dear children, they always see God."

Read to the children the angel poems, "I Wish I Could See the Bright Angel," and "When Little Children Wake at Morn," — M. Mannix.

Review the story of the angels from day to day in connection with the following activities:

a) Make a special study of the art pictures of angels. Mount them and expose them to the children's view all week.

b) Have the children dramatize any phase of child life in some way connected with the angel; e.g., child prayer while the guardian angel hovers over him; studying with the angel near by. Let the groups select any situation which is appropriate. (Warning to the teacher: Do not make important any physical protection of the angel. There is no ecclesiastical approval of these situations.)

c) Angel Booklet: The children may collect their pictures and arrange the booklet as they wish. Display these in the classroom; the children will offer them as gifts to parents.

d) Creative Art: Paper cutting or clay modeling of angels.

e) Have the children find in various first-grade readers, stories about the angels and tell them to each other in a socialized period. This activity is for the second semester only.

f) For other suggestions, see *The Little Ones,* pages 16 to 25.

Teacher's References:

The Holy Bible, Matthew, Chapter IV.

The Little Ones, pages 16 to 25, "The Angels."

Practical Aids, page 13, "The Smile of Your Guardian Angel."

To the Heart of the Child, Lesson III, "The Angels."

Catholic School Journal, September, 1931, "The Guardian Angels."

Teacher's Notes:

My Best Friend
October, 4th Week; February, 4th Week

Introduction:

Sing a hymn to Jesus.

Presentation:

"God is so good to you. He made you; He gave you kind parents and friends. Your best friends on earth are your mother and father. But God did something still more wonderful for you. He loved you so much that He sent Jesus, His own Son, down to earth. Jesus is the Son of God. He came to be your Best Friend. He loved you more than your good mother and father can love you. Jesus shows you how to be good and happy. If you are good, Jesus, your Best Friend, the Son of God, will take you to heaven some day, to be happy with Him forever."

Study the picture on page 19. Stress the love of Jesus for each one of them. Jesus is saying to them: "Come to Me. I am your Best Friend." Read the lesson.

Study the picture on page 20, *The Good Shepherd*. Tell the children that they are Jesus' little sheep; that mother and father are His big sheep. He loves all His sheep and is leading them all to heaven. A good little sheep always stays near Jesus. Let them imagine they are one of the sheep in the picture. Ask them how they can stay near Jesus always. Let them talk freely about the picture.

Teacher's Notes:

UNIT IV

THE NATIVITY: PRE-CHRISTMAS SEASON

The Announcement to Zachary
November, 1st Week; March, 1st Week

Introduction:

"The time was coming nearer and nearer when God would send His own Son to live with men on earth. Many years had passed since God had promised Him to Adam and Eve. Why did God promise to send His own dear Son to this earth?"

Repeat briefly the story of the fall of Adam and Eve and God's promise to send them a Redeemer. Stress the goodness of God.

Presentation:

"A long time ago a Jewish priest and his wife Elizabeth lived in a little town near Jerusalem. Zachary was the name of this priest. They were very good, holy people. They loved God and often prayed that He would send His Son down to earth soon. They knew that God had promised this to Adam and Eve. They knew that the Son of God would come down to earth to show the people how to live and to open the gates of heaven again. You see, it was many thousand years since God had made this promise and all the Jews longed for the Son of God.

"One day Zachary, the priest of the Jews, was praying to God in the temple, asking God to send His Son soon. While he was at prayer, suddenly a beautiful angel stood before him. Zachary was frightened, but the angel said to him: 'Fear not, Zachary, for your prayer is heard. You and Elizabeth shall have a son. You shall call his name John. He shall be great before the Lord.'

"Zachary said to the angel: 'How shall I know this?' Then the angel spoke once more to him: 'I am Gabriel, who stand before

44

the Lord. God sent me to bring you the good news. Because you did not believe my words, you will not be able to speak until everything has happened as I told you.' Then the angel left Zachary. When Zachary came out of the temple, he could not say a word. He could not speak again until their little son was born and until they had called him John."

Show the picture, *The Angel and Zachary*. Retell the story through the study of the picture. Let a few of the children step before the class, take the picture, and tell the others all they know about it.

The Birth of John
November, 1st Week; March, 1st Week

Introduction:

Review the previous lesson by a dramatization of the angel's appearance to Zachary. Let the children use their own words. One child tells the story until the conversation takes place between the angel and Zachary. Then two other children take the parts. Let this be repeated quite frequently by different groups until the story is known by all. Make the dumbness of Zachary quite prominent.

Presentation:

"Zachary could not speak. He had to write the wonderful news on a writing tablet for Elizabeth. When Elizabeth heard that God was sending her a son, she was very happy. This boy was to be great before the Lord. He was to prepare the way of the Lord. Now Zachary and Elizabeth knew that God would soon send His own Son to earth. Their little boy would grow up into a strong man. He would tell the people that God had kept His promise to Adam and Eve; that He had sent His own Son on earth to open heaven for them once more."

Tell the story of the birth of John.

Dramatize the naming of the child John.

Teacher's References:

Gospel of St. Luke. All of Chapter I.

Leading the Little Ones to Christ, "The Savior's Coming Announced," pages 73–79.

Teacher's Notes:

The Annunciation
November, 2nd Week; March, 1st Week

Introduction:

"Thousands and thousands of years ago God made heaven and earth. Heaven is the home of God. It is the most beautiful place that God could make. God wanted Adam and Eve and all their children, everybody who would ever live on this earth, to come to heaven sometime. But Adam and Eve disobeyed God and the gates of heaven were closed. Only the Son of God could open them again. To do this, He had to become man and live on this earth. He had to save all the people from the devil. That is why He is called the Savior."

Explain the word Savior by telling a little story in which a child has been saved from drowning, being run over, or any other similar event. Tell how the one who saved the child is called his savior from death. Jesus is the greatest Savior because He has saved us from our sins and opened heaven for us all.

Presentation:

"Now the time was near when God wanted to send His Son to save all men. God had millions and millions of most wonderful angels in heaven. He sent one of the grandest angels, Gabriel, to be His messenger to earth. You remember Gabriel had also been sent by God to Zachary.

"God sent the Angel Gabriel to a little town called Nazareth. Here lived a lovely lady. Her heart was so pure and good that God loved her more than anyone else on earth. The beautiful lady's name was Mary. Mary lived in a little house in Nazareth with St. Joseph, her spouse. Mary had prayed and prayed that the Savior would soon be born. One day while she was praying, the Angel Gabriel stood before her and said: 'Hail, Mary, full of Grace, the Lord is with thee: blessed art thou amongst women!' "

Explain that the courtesy of the angel toward the Blessed Virgin should teach us how to show respect toward God, toward the Blessed Virgin, toward our Guardian Angel, by saying our prayers to them reverently, by kneeling or standing straight at prayer, by folding our hands properly.

"Mary became frightened, but the Angel said to her: 'Fear not, Mary.' Then he told her a most wonderful secret. He told her that God wanted to come down from heaven now, wanted to become a tiny Baby, and she, Mary, should be His Mother. She should call His name Jesus."

Teach the children to bow their heads slightly whenever they pronounce or hear others pronounce the Holy Name of Jesus. If there is any need for calling attention in the class to the abuse of the Holy Name, do it here; if not, it is better not to suggest the misuse of it.

"It was all so wonderful that Mary did not know what to say. The angel told her that God could do anything, that He wanted her to be His own Mother. Mary was afraid. But the angel of the Lord said: 'The Holy Ghost shall come upon thee.' Mary was very happy and said to the angel: 'Behold the handmaid of the Lord.' She meant that she would do what God wanted. She would obey. Then Jesus, the Son of God, came down from heaven into the beautiful heart of Mary. God, the Holy Ghost, had filled Mary's soul with love. The Angel Gabriel had returned to heaven to tell the wonderful story of Mary, the holy virgin. Mary was so happy. She kept on saying in her heart: 'God is coming to earth. He will be a tiny Baby. I am going to be His Mother. Oh! I love Him so much. I hope all the people and the little children will love Him, too.' "

Show the picture of the Annunciation. It would be most advantageous to have a wall picture of the Annunciation before the class throughout the study of this lesson. (Perhaps an interchange of pictures between classrooms might be suggested here, this being done as the occasions develop.) The teacher repeats the story first, while using the picture. Then the children tell it again and again, referring to the figures on the picture while they are telling the story. Be sure to repeat the exact words, for in that way the Hail Mary and the Angelus can be learned incidentally. Some time during this week, the Hail Mary should be taught as a prayer. For suggestions how to teach the Hail Mary, consult *The Little Ones,* by M. Eaton, pages 36–42.

Introduction:

Show any picture of the Annunciation. Repeat the story through a study of the picture. Let the children talk freely about it. Try to have them use the exact Scriptural texts.

"Did God know what Mary was saying in her heart? How did He know? Do you think God loved to hear Mary say, 'I love You'? Does God know what you are thinking? Would God like you to tell Him that you love Him? Tell Jesus now very quietly in your heart that you love Him. Often during the day whisper to Jesus, 'O Jesus, I love You.' Often whisper to Mary, too: 'O Mary, I love you. You are my Mother in heaven.' "

In a dramatization of the Annunciation let the pupils be most free in their actions as well as in their words. However, it is very good for them to use the quotations, as they form the very prayers they will say all their lives.

Presentation:

Let this be the dramatization of the angel's visit to Mary. A little girl, wearing a veil on her head, is the Blessed Virgin; one of the other children is the angel. To make it a little more realistic, fasten some wings made of gauzy material to the angel. Let the other children be the angels in heaven, to whom Gabriel tells his story of the visit to Mary. If the children know a hymn to Mary let them sing or hum it softly while the angel is with Mary.

Other activities through which the story can be repeated:

a) Build on the sand table the hillside of Nazareth. Show the home of Mary. Cut out a picture of Mary, of an angel. Mount them on heavy cardboard, and cut out again, or just place a support of cardboard on these pictures. Cut-outs and silhouettes can be purchased at Co-op Parish Activities Service, Effingham, Ill.

b) Place them in the home of Mary in such positions as to represent the Annunciation.

c) Let the children color the outline pictures which the teacher can hectograph. Cut and mount them for a poster. For a poster suggestion on the Annunciation, consult *Practical Aids,* page 289.

Study the picture in *The Book of the Holy Child* and read the lesson, page 21.

Teach the following prayers:

The Hail Mary. This prayer will be the chief prayer throughout the Christmas season. It can best be learned in this lesson on the Annunciation.

The Angelus, as a prayer, will be studied in the second semester, when the lesson on the Annunciation is repeated in connection with *The Book of the Holy Child.* The sections of the Angelus should be studied quite slowly so that all the children will understand what they are saying.

Study the picture and read the lessons, pages 23 and 24.

Have the children memorize the following poem and quotations:

> "An angel came to Mary's house —
>   It was a holy place,
> He bowed his head and whispered low,
>   Hail, Mary, full of grace."
>   — *A School Sister of Notre Dame*

"Hail, full of grace, the Lord is with thee" (Luke i. 28).
"Blessed art thou among women" (Luke i. 28).

Teacher's References:

Gospel of St. Luke, i. 26–39.
Gospel of St. Matthew, i. 18–25.

Leading the Little Ones to Christ, "The Savior's Coming Announced," pages 73–78.

The Little Ones, "The Annunciation," page 216; Poster of the Annunciation, page 289; "The Hail Mary," pages 36 and 68.

Practical Aids, "Feast of the Annunciation," page 215; Poster of the Annunciation, page 289.

Teacher Tells a Story, "The Hail Mary," pages 88–94.

Teacher's Notes:

Mary's Visit to Elizabeth
November, 3rd Week; March, 1st Week

Introduction:

Let a child come before the class and tell again the story of the Annunciation, or let the simple dramatization take place again.

Review the lesson by means of questions like the following, children finding the answers in the book and reading them aloud, page 21:

When the angel came to Mary, what did he say to her? Why did God love Mary so much that He asked her to be His Mother? What did Mary tell the angel? How did Mary feel when she heard that God wanted her to be His very own Mother?

Presentation:

"Mary was very happy when she heard the good news about the Baby Jesus coming to earth. Elizabeth, the wife of Zachary, was the cousin of Mary. Mary loved her cousin, Elizabeth, and went to help her prepare for the birth of her little son, John.

Elizabeth lived far away from Nazareth. When she saw Mary coming, she went out to meet her. Elizabeth, who was soon to be the mother of John, knelt down before the Holy Mary and cried in a loud voice, 'Blessed art thou among women and blessed is the Fruit of thy womb.' And Mary sang a most beautiful song about God, and how good He is to His people."

Read *The Book of the Holy Child*, "Hail Mary," page 24.

Study the picture, *The Visitation,* by Albertinelli, if it is available. The pictures from *The Sacred Heart Messenger* can be mounted and kept in view of the children on the bulletin boards. Review the story through the picture.

"After Mary had finished speaking, the priest Zachary, the husband of Elizabeth, knelt before her. He could not speak. Who can tell me why Zachary could not speak?"

Repeat the story of Zachary and the Angel.

Speak of Mary's three months' visit; of her charity, her love for her relatives, of her longing for the birth of Jesus.

"Everybody at Elizabeth's house was made happy by Mary. You see, she was full of grace. God, the Holy Ghost, had made her so good and beautiful. Do you try to make people happy? What can you do to make your dear mother happy? your father? your little brothers and sisters?

Discuss with the children many little home scenes in which they can show their love for their parents, for their sisters and brothers. Kindness, charity, unselfishness, respect are virtues which could be talked about; however, this must all be done on the child's level. Present little problems which occur in the child's daily life; ask them to be the judge in each problem.

Home at Nazareth

Introduction:

Repeat the story of the visit through a dramatization somewhat like the following:

SCENE I: The Blessed Virgin arrives at the home of Elizabeth. Let this be a corner of the room near the door. Elizabeth comes through the door to meet her. She kneels down before Mary, holds out her arms to her and says:

"Blessed art thou among women. Mary, my dear cousin, you are the Mother of God and you come to me!"

Mary folds her hands in prayer, looks up to heaven and says: "The Lord God be praised!"

Then she takes Elizabeth by the hands and they walk to the door. Zachary comes in at the same door and kneels down before Mary. He shows by signs to Mary that he cannot speak. Mary blesses him by putting her hands on his head. The three walk into the house.

Presentation:

"Mary stayed with Elizabeth for three months. She helped Elizabeth get ready for the coming of her little son, John. Now Mary knew that her own little Son was soon coming to be her Baby. She said good-by and started on her way home to Nazareth, back to dear St. Joseph. He was waiting so long for her to come home.

"One night after Mary came home, God sent one of His lovely angels to Joseph. Joseph was asleep in his little room. Suddenly the room became bright as day and Joseph in a dream saw the angel. The angel told St. Joseph that the Savior was coming soon; that Mary would be His Mother. The angel said: 'She shall bring forth a Son: and thou shalt call His Name Jesus. For He shall save His people from their sins.' Then the angel left and St. Joseph knelt down and thanked God. How much God loved St. Joseph. St. Joseph was to be the foster father of the Infant Jesus. How much Jesus loved St. Joseph!'"

Teach the children to say very often a little prayer to St. Joseph. Tell them how good St. Joseph is and that he loves them and will help them if they pray to him.

Sing a song to St. Joseph.

Teacher's References:

A Child's Garden of Religion Stories, "Mary's Visit to Elizabeth," page 166.

The Little Ones, "The First Half of the Hail Mary," page 86.
Gospel of St. Matthew, i. 16–25.
Gospel of St. Luke. All of Chapter I.

Teacher's Notes:

The Journey
November, 3rd and 4th Weeks; March, 1st Week

Introduction:

Sing a song to Mary.

Review briefly the previous lessons through questions:

What did the Angel Gabriel say to Mary when he visited her? Why did he bow before her? Who told the angel to go to Mary? What did Mary answer the angel? Where did Mary go to tell her wonderful secret? Who told St. Joseph about the Baby Jesus? Why did God want St. Joseph to take care of Mary and the Baby Jesus? Why did the Baby Jesus come on earth?

Read the text, pages 21 to 24.

Presentation:

"The Blessed Virgin Mary and St. Joseph lived in their little home in Nazareth. They worked and prayed. They prayed that God would soon send His Son Jesus to them and to the whole earth.

"One day, not long after Mary had come home from her visit to Elizabeth, Joseph hastened home from his work to tell Mary something. He said to Mary: 'We must go to Bethlehem. The king wants to count his people.' The sweet Virgin Mary said: 'Let us obey the king. It is God's will.' The way was far, but Mary and Joseph got ready at once. All they could take with them was a little bundle of clothes for themselves and for the little Baby Jesus. Mary knew that God would send Jesus to her when they would reach Bethlehem. Mary and Joseph were very poor. Mary rode on a little donkey and St. Joseph walked next to her. St. Joseph always took good care of Mary, because God wanted him to. He knew that God loved Mary and wanted her to be the Mother of His own Son, Jesus. St. Joseph loved Mary very, very much."

Study the pictures on pages 25 to 27. Read "Home at Nazareth," page 25.

Tell the story of the hard trip to Bethlehem, how Joseph and Mary often had to let the wealthy pass them on the road; how there was no room for them; how finally they were directed to the cave.

Show the picture *No Room for Them in the Inn*, by Merson. Repeat the story from day to day through a study of the picture. Pin it on the bulletin board at eye level of the children.

Introduction:

Read to the children the lesson, "The Journey," pages 26 to 29.

Dramatize the Journey to Bethlehem.

Let the children dramatize this lesson in three scenes.

SCENE I: Joseph comes home and tells the Blessed Virgin Mary about the edict. Her answer to him and their departure closes the scene. The Blessed Virgin should wear a veil and carry a little bundle; St. Joseph carries a staff.

SCENE II. Joseph and Mary are on their way. Let the children accompany them. They all march around the room a few times with music; or the children may hum a hymn.

SCENE III: Joseph and Mary arrive in Bethlehem. Some of the children are grouped in various parts of the room to represent the inhabitants of Bethlehem. Joseph stops at each group and asks for a room. They answer that they have no room. And so from one group to another, until one man tells them of the cave. St. Joseph thanks him and they start for the cave.

The sand table can now be arranged. For the present lesson, arrange it in the form of a hilly country. Let there be one prominent path leading to Bethlehem and many little side paths for the sheep. Arrange sheep and shepherds over the hillsides. Have statues or figures of Mary and Joseph, coming down the road. Change the position of the figures from day to day; also that of the sheep.

Show the city of Bethlehem by making a few houses from cardboard. Show the hillside beyond Bethlehem and the cave.

Presentation:

"Think of it, dear children! Nobody in the little town would take in Mother Mary and St. Joseph. Poor Mary, she was so tired. Poor Joseph, he felt so sorry for Mary. Poor little Jesus wanted to be born that night and nobody would let His holy Mother come in. Now suppose you had lived in Bethlehem, would you have let them come into your house? What would you have said? What would you have done? How could you have made Mary and Joseph happy?"

At this point speak to the children on little acts of obedience at home, in school, which they must do because it is God's will for them. Let them suggest how they can perform little acts of charity for the love of Jesus. Teacher adds her own suggestions.

Read the lesson "Rose and Her Mother" in the text, page 30.

In case a teacher does not care to use the sand table, she may build a stable in one corner of the classroom and follow the directions given in *Practical Aids* on page 90. Keep the children at this Christmas project throughout the month of December, spiritualizing it by suggestion of virtues to be practiced by the children in connection with it. For example (adapted from *Practical Aids*), the class could make a bed for the Holy Infant as follows:

Bedstead — Masses attended.

Mattress — Acts of Obedience.

Spring — Acts of Kindness.

Sheets — Acts of Contrition.

Blankets — Acts of Unselfishness.

Pillows — Acts of Longing for Jesus.

Other things could be added, such as sheep, ox, floor, roof, by performing little virtuous acts suggested by the children.

Close the lesson with one oral reading, pages 26 to 29, by the children. Let one child read the explanatory parts and others the character parts.

At the regular singing period teach the children the simple Christmas hymns, such as "Dear Little One," "Holy Night," "Lovely Infant."

The little prayer, "Infant Jesus, Bless Us," should be added to each school prayer.

The poem, "Gifts," by Christina Rosetti, can be taught in the oral-expression class during the week. This poem is also set to music. See *The Child's Song Treasury*, by Mary B. Ehrmann.

Teacher's References:

Practical Aids, sand-table project, "Bethlehem," page 231; "Exercises in Preparation for Christmas," page 90; "Mary and Joseph on Their Way to Bethlehem," page 95; "No Room for Them in the Inn," page 96.

Teacher Tells a Story, Vol. II, "Obedience to Authority," pages 110–141; "Helping the Poor," pages 99–109.

A Child's Garden of Religion Stories, "The Birth of Our King," pages 168–172.

The Little Ones, "The Journey to Bethlehem," page 28; "Suggestions on How to Make a Crib," page 30.

Teacher's Notes:

UNIT V

THE NATIVITY: CHRISTMAS SEASON

The First Christmas
December, 1st Week; March, 2nd Week

The Book of the Holy Child, Part IV, "The First Christmas," page 32.

Introduction I:

The teacher has arranged one corner of the room as the stable of Bethlehem — the larger, the better. In it she has placed a crib with straw, in which lies a statue of the Infant Jesus. Statues of Mary, Joseph, animals are grouped about the crib. If the figures are small, it would be better to place the crib on a table. Have an electric light arranged so as to produce the best effect upon the crib. All should be arranged in such a way as to remain in the classroom throughout the Christmas season, to the time when the lesson on The Flight Into Egypt is begun. The entire arrangement should be made as beautiful as possible. So that the children will not see it before the psychological moment, let it be screened off in some way.

Review Questions:

What did the people of Bethlehem say to Mary and Joseph? Did they know that Mary was to be the Mother of Jesus, their Savior? Who knew about it? Where did they find a place for the night?

Let us read about the journey once more, page 26.

Presentation:

"When the man had said to Joseph and Mary: 'There is a stable on the side of that hill. I keep my oxen and cattle there. You may stay there.' Joseph and Mary thanked him and started

57

up the hill. Poor Mary and Joseph! They were so tired! Soon they reached the stable. What a poor place it was for them and for the little Baby Jesus who was coming that very night. The oxen and sheep were asleep. St. Joseph helped the Blessed Virgin off the donkey. Then he tied the animal near the oxen and began to make the stable clean and warm. He laid fresh straw on the floor for the Blessed Virgin's bed; and he also put clean straw into the manger. This would be the bed for Baby Jesus. It was almost time for Jesus to come.

"It was a cold, still night. The people in Bethlehem were all asleep. The stars were twinkling as if they knew something beautiful was going to happen. It was midnight, dark, dark, dark. Close your eyes, children, be very still." (Teacher pulls the shades to darken the room, quietly removes the screen. Let some of the older children of the school, dressed as angels, enter the room very quietly and sing softly while they group themselves about the crib. They should not obstruct the view of the children. The crib is lighted. The angels finish their song, adore the Infant, and leave as they have entered. Sister will continue the story at) "Mother Mary adored the Son of God, her Baby Boy, for He was God. Then she took Him into her arms. She was so happy. She knew the lovely Baby in her arms was her own dear little Boy and God, too.

"Sweet Mother Mary put little Jesus into the crib. Angels came from heaven and sang: 'Glory to God in the highest.' Mother Mary and St. Joseph knelt down and thanked the Baby Jesus for coming down from heaven. Dear children, kneel down and say very softly: 'Thank You, Baby Jesus, for coming to us. We love You so much.'" Now let the children sing softly all the little Christmas hymns and songs to Mary.

Learn the Christmas song, "Why Do Bells for Christmas Ring?" during the regular singing periods.

Introduction:

Sister reads in a beautiful manner from *The Book of the Holy Child,* "The First Christmas," page 32, and "Little Child in the Crib," page 33.

The following dramatization entitled "A Moment of Silence,"[1] is very effective:

Tell the children to sit very still, "With feet still, body still, arms still, head still" (Dr. Montessori). Darken the room, turn on the light at the crib. The children close their eyes for a little while. Sister says: I will be Mother Mary. When I call your name come to the crib and very softly say to Jesus, "Jesus, Jesus, my little God," or any other little prayer you want to. Sister goes behind the crib and calls one child after the other very softly, just in a whisper. When all the children have been called and are at the crib, they once more sing a Christmas hymn. The teacher will recite to Baby Jesus the poem on page 33.

The children can also be told to do what they like at the crib for the Baby Jesus; e.g., sing, read, or recite the little poem, page 33, or say a prayer.

Presentation:

The story should be repeated from day to day until each child knows and can tell it. However, the main idea to be kept in mind is: Jesus' love for the child; the child's love for Jesus. The children can show their love for Jesus by little acts of charity, little prayers, by study, by gentleness. Let the children suggest every morning one special act that they will all perform each day of Advent for love of the Infant Jesus and in preparation for Christmas. The teacher should remind them of it frequently during the day. This is called their Spiritual Crib. All activities can be turned into a prayer as a preparation for Christmas.

The children should be taught to prepare their hearts as a little crib for the Baby Jesus on Christmas morning. This they can do by performing little sacrifices, saving their pennies to help buy heathen babies for Jesus, eat what Mother wants them to eat, take care of the baby.

Each child can make its own little crib for Baby Jesus by cutting cribs from paper, setting them up in a clean paper box. They can fill the manger with straw, fine paper cuttings, for every little act they have performed for Jesus. Pictures of the Blessed

---

[1] Adapted from *The Little Ones* (page 46), by Mary Eaton. By permission of B. Herder Book Company, publishers.

Virgin and St. Joseph and the Infant can be cut from cards and catalogs and pasted into the box. They can also cut sheep. Inexpensive cut-outs may be obtained from Co-op Parish Activities Service, Effingham, Ill.

As the story of Christmas progresses, let the children continue the sand-table project.

Let the children look at the Christmas pictures which have been mounted and placed about the room at the children's eye level. Make a special study on one day of the picture preferred.

The hymn, "Come, Gather Here, Children," should be learned during this week. While the children sing it, if room permits, let them stand near the crib; otherwise let various groups take turns around the crib. Have the children sing these beautiful Christmas hymns very often, devoutly, softly.

Teach the children the poems on pages 33 and 38 of the text. Let them step before the crib singly and recite the poems to the Infant Jesus as soon as they know them. This may also be in way of reward for beautiful conduct.

The teacher will recite "Jesus Answers from the Crib," text, page 38, in answer to each child who recites the first poem on page 38. When any one of the children knows this poem also, let him give the answer.

Each child will memorize the quotation through the song, "Glory to God in the Highest and Peace to Men of Good Will."

The following Christmas poems will be taken with the children during their expression or English class:

"Out of Bounds" — Father Tabb.

"Christmas" — Anonymous.

"Like One I Know" — Nancy Campbell.

"Christmas Night" — Father Faber.

"Christmas Carol" — Sara Teasdale.

If available, the teacher might also use the picture, *The Nativity*, by Feuerstein; and *Holy Night*, by Correggio, would make a nice wall picture in connection with this lesson.

Pupil's Readings:

American First Reader, "The Children's Christmas," page 50; "A Great Birthday," page 51.

Corona Primer, "Christmas," page 119.

Corona First Reader, "The Birth of Our Lord," page 53.

A table can be arranged with books and pictures to which the children should have free access all through the study of this unit.

Teacher's References:

The Little Ones, "Bethlehem," page 28; "A Moment of Silence," page 46.

Art Education Through Religion I, "Paper Cutting, Crib," page 18.

Practical Aids, "The Feast of Christmas," page 83; "Why Jesus Came Down Upon Earth," page 84; "Unselfishness of Jesus in the Crib," page 85; "A Child's Preparation for Christmas," page 89; "Pious Exercises in Preparation for Christmas," page 90.

To the Heart of the Child, "The Birth of the Messias," page 46.

A Child's Garden of Religion Stories, "The Savior is Born," page 176.

Leading the Little Ones to Christ, "The Savior is Born to Us," pages 79–85.

Teacher's Notes:

The Announcement
December, 2nd Week; March, 2nd Week

Pictures:

The Announcement — Plockhorst.

The Arrival of the Shepherds — Lerolle.

Adoration of the Shepherds — Murillo.

Wall Picture:

The Announcement — Plockhorst.

Introduction:

Sing a hymn to the Infant Jesus.

Children repeat the story of the "Journey and the Birth of Our Lord" briefly, using the pictures of the previous lessons. Then read the poem again on page 33.

Presentation:

"When Jesus was born in Bethlehem on Christmas Night, some poor shepherds were out in the field taking care of their sheep. Most of the men were sleeping."

Let the children arrange the sand table to illustrate the country near Bethlehem; sheep, tent, shepherds on the hills in different positions; the cave of Bethlehem off to the side. While the children are arranging the table, let them repeat the story again and again.

"Suddenly they were awakened by a beautiful light in the sky. Jesus had sent His angels to these shepherds. Happy and glorious angels were singing to these poor shepherds about the Infant Jesus. One of the angels said to them: 'Fear not, I bring you tidings of great joy. This day is born to you a Savior, who is Christ the Lord, in the city of David. You shall find the Infant wrapped in swaddling clothes, and laid in a manger.' Then the whole army of angels sang in the sweetest tones: 'Glory to God in the highest; and on earth peace to men of good will' " (Luke ii. 14).

Teach the strains, "Glory to God in the Highest," as found in the old Christmas hymns.

Continue the songs of Christmas.

"The shepherds were very happy. They said: 'Let us go over to Bethlehem.' They ran to the poor stable. There they found the Baby Jesus, their God, with His Mother Mary and St. Joseph. And they fell down upon their knees, and adored Jesus. Then the dear little Jesus whispered something beautiful into the hearts of these poor shepherds. After a little while, they went back home and told the wonderful story to their children."

Show the picture, *The Angels and the Shepherds,* by Plock-horst. Let the children repeat the story through the picture study.

Show the picture, *Arrival of the Shepherds,* by Lerolle, and *The Adoration of the Shepherds,* by Murillo. Always repeat the story while studying the pictures.

All these pictures should be kept in view of the children throughout the season. During oral-expression classes, let them select the picture they like best and tell the story to the class.

Introduction:

Read *The Book of the Holy Child:* "The Announcement," pages 34–37, and study the pictures of the text carefully.

Dramatization of the coming of the shepherds.

Dramatize the scenes of the shepherds hearing the news; hastening to the crib; adoring at the crib. Again let the children be free to speak and act as they will. Tell them it would be very beautiful if they could use some of the exact words of the angels. See *Practical Aids,* "Dramatization of the Adoration of Shepherds," page 242.

Presentation:

"The shepherds were very poor people. Jesus loved them because they were good. The shepherds came again and again to see the Baby Jesus. They often brought little boys and girls along, too. Mother Mary would let the shepherds and the little children hold Jesus. Jesus smiled on them and blessed them. The shepherds knew that tiny little Baby was God. Do you think they brought Him any gifts? If you had been one of those little children, could you have brought Baby Jesus a gift? Where can you visit Jesus every day if you want to? What gift can you give Him?"

Read *The Book of the Holy Child:* "Child and Infant Jesus," page 38; "Robert's Gift," page 39.

Teach the poem, "A Song," by Charles L. O'Donnell; read it to the children day by day, with simplicity and love.

The teacher will speak to the children of the virtues practiced by the Infant Jesus, such as poverty, charity, unselfishness, gentleness, kindness to the poor. She will encourage them to practice some of these through specific acts in preparation for Christmas. Let the children suggest what they wish to do and for each act if they have made a little crib, let them place their piece of straw in it. This crib might be their Christmas gift to their parents.

Creative Art: Have each child draw any scene he likes in the story. Even though it may be quite crude, still praise the child. Let him give his drawing to the Baby Jesus in the crib.

Cut angels from paper and color them. Paste them as a border at the top of the blackboard.

Teach the hymn, "Baby Jesus Smiling"; also repeat the other hymns of Christmas from day to day. At times let the children fold their hands when they sing a hymn and kneel around the crib.

The Aspiration: "Infant, Jesus, bless us," can be written or printed on the board.

The following quotations might be written on the board: "Glory to God in the highest; and on earth peace to men of good will" (Luke ii. 14).

"Fear not, for, behold, I bring you tidings of great joy" (Luke ii. 10).

"For, this day, is born to you a Savior, who is Christ the Lord, in the city of David" (Luke ii. 11).

While the teacher tells the story again and again, she should use the above Biblical quotations, stating them very slowly. Soon the children can repeat the words. Have the children use them in their repetition of the stories.

Pupil's Readings:

Corona First Reader, "The Birth of Our Lord," page 53.

Rosary Primer, "The Best Gift," page 74.

Ideal Catholic Reader, "The Shepherds," page 38.

Teacher's References:

The Holy Bible.

Practical Aids, "Unselfishness of Jesus in the Crib," page 85; "The Selfishness of Some Children," page 86; "The Shepherds Hasten to the Crib," page 97; "Longing for Jesus," page 98.

The Little Ones, "The Shepherds," pages 42–44.

Child's Garden of Religion Stories, "Angels from Heaven," pages 180–186.

Jesus of Nazareth, Mother Loyola, "The First Christmas Night," page 61.

Leading the Little Ones to Christ, "Childhood Friends of Jesus: The Wise Men," pages 97–103.

Teacher's Notes:

Review
December, 3rd and 4th Week

The remaining time before Christmas should be spent in reviewing the complete story of the Nativity. The crib, posters, sand-table projects, hymns, poems, should be brought to a finish so that the children may enjoy them to the fullest. Encourage the children to prepare very well this last week, because the Infant Jesus wants to come into their hearts on Christmas during Mass. Explain to the children how Jesus comes into the hearts of people on Christmas morning when they go to Holy Communion. The children themselves are not old enough yet to receive Jesus in Holy Communion, but if they pray very hard to Jesus on Christmas morning, "Infant Jesus, come to me. I love You!" Jesus will bless them. Instill in the children a longing to receive Jesus soon in Holy Communion. Tell them to give Jesus their little hearts on Christmas by praying to Him, by reciting their little poems to Him.

Review of the stories: Have the children, one by one, come

before the class, with picture in hand, and tell the class the corresponding story.

For the last school day before Christmas, the teacher will re-arrange the crib in the front of the room; place a well-loaded Christmas tree near it. A program consisting of the hymns, poems, stories the children have been studying, should take place, in which each child takes part.

Suggested Program:

Hymn: "Come, Gather Here, Children."

The Annunciation (one child tell the story, showing the picture).

The Visitation (one child tell the story, showing the picture).

The Journey, a small group dramatize this story.

The Birth, a child tells the story.

Hymn, "Dear Little One."

Poems: "A Little Child at the Crib"; "Jesus Answers from the Crib" (one child recites and another child answers).

Coming of the Shepherds (group dramatizes this while children softly hum or sing, "Glory to God").

Poem or Song: "Gifts."

Hymn: "Lovely Infant," during which a few children stand before the crib and tinkle little Christmas bells.

Distribution of gifts from the tree.

Christ is Brought to the Temple
January, 1st Week; March, 3rd Week

Introduction:

Tell the children when they were little babies, God wished their parents to bring them to Church and to offer them to Him. Ever since then God wants them always to be near to Him.

Presentation:

"Once when Jesus was still a tiny Baby His Mother Mary and St. Joseph brought Him to the temple to offer Him to God. St. Joseph brought two doves as an offering to God the Father.

"There was a holy old man named Simeon in the temple. He knew that Jesus would soon be coming to earth. He had waited for Jesus many years. He was in the temple when Mary and Joseph came in with Baby Jesus. When Simeon saw them, he went up to Mother Mary. She put little Jesus into his old arms. Simeon wept for joy because he now saw Jesus."

Study the picture, *The Presentation*, by Carpaccio.

"He thanked God and said: 'Now Thou dost dismiss Thy servant, O Lord, according to Thy word in peace' (Luke ii. 29). He meant that now he was ready to die, because he had seen Jesus. There was a very old lady in the temple. She, too, took the little Jesus into her arms and thanked God that the Savior had come. The old Simeon called Jesus the Light of the World."

Show the children the picture, *The Light of the World*, by Chambers. Speak about the Child Jesus being their light because He whispers to them so often in their hearts to be good and not to do what is wrong.

Tell them that the candles burning on the altar tell us that Jesus is the Light of the World.

"Then Mary and Joseph offered Jesus to God. Jesus was the most wonderful Gift God had ever received. Next to Jesus, God wants you. How can you give yourself to God?"

Discuss with the children what little gifts they can give to God every day: Their hearts, by keeping them pure; their actions, by saying, "All for You, O Jesus"; their thoughts by always thinking beautiful things and often thinking of Jesus. At Mass they should offer themselves to God. Talk, too, on the penny offerings little children should make on Sundays to Jesus.

Read: *The Book of the Holy Child*, "My Wish," page 50. The teacher will read this to the class.

Review: *The Book of the Holy Child*, "O Sweetest Jesus," page 38.

"The Holy Family went back home. The Blessed Mother and St. Joseph took good care of little Jesus and loved Him better day by day."

Let the children repeat the story in connection with the following activities:

a) Paper cutting: a candle, doves, dove cage.

b) Clay model: a candle, dove, dove cage.

c) Read the poem, "Gifts," by Julia Johnson Davis. Discuss it with the class.

d) Learn the hymn, "Mary Mother of God."

e) Oral talks on what I saw in the Temple; what was said in the Temple.

f) End the study of this lesson with a procession.

g) Dramatization: A little girl, with a veil on her head, is Mary. A little boy, staff in hand, St. Joseph. Simeon and Anna walk very slowly. Children follow in procession holding candles they have made.

Scenes: Mary and Joseph leave Bethlehem, Mary carries the Infant. Let the little girl carry the statue of the Child Jesus. They, followed by the children with their candles, walk slowly around the room. When they reach the temple, one corner of the room, Simeon and old Anna meet them. Mary gives the Babe in turn to each. Simeon's words could be the quotation in the lesson; Anna thanks God for the Savior. Teacher's desk can be arranged as the altar; the priest, one of the boys, takes the Infant and placing Him on the altar, offers Him to God. Mary also offers Him. St. Joseph gives the doves in exchange for the Child. They return home, put the Baby back into the crib, and end with the song, "Gifts" and other Christmas songs.

h) Pictures that might be studied are:

The Presentation — Carpaccio.

The Light of the World — Chambers.

Pupil's Readings:

Corona First Reader, "Simeon and the Holy Child," page 124.

Teacher's References:

Practical Aids, "Poster Design," page 290; "How to Cut Out Doves, Camels, Donkey," page 270; "The Purification of the Blessed Virgin," page 211.

The Holy Bible, St. Luke, Chapter II; "Jesus of Nazareth." "In the Temple," Chapter 9.

Leading the Little Ones to Christ, "Childhood Friend of Jesus"; "Simeon and Anna," pages 103–109.

Teacher's Notes:

Christ in the Arms of His Mother
January, 1st Week

To the Teacher:

This is a special lesson, the aim of which is to increase in the child its love for Mary, the Mother of God. As many pictures as possible, with one beautiful wall picture of the Blessed Virgin and the Child, should be placed in the room, and the children permitted to examine them as they wish. Special attention should be •called to them, and during the oral-expression classes, they should form the topic for the children.

Introduction:

Show the children any of the following pictures and study especially the wall picture:

Madonna of the Chair — Raphael.

Sistine Madonna — Raphael.

Madonna and Child, by any of the following artists: Sichel, Deger, Ittenbach, Bodenhausen, Dagnan, Dolci.

Whom do you see in this picture? Do you think Mother Mary loves little Jesus very much? Does Jesus love His Mother very much, too? How does He show His love?

Presentation:

"See how happy little Jesus looks in Mother Mary's arms. She loves Him, oh, so much. Jesus knows just how much she loves Him, because He is God. He knows all things. He knows how much you love Him and His holy Mother, too. Jesus and Mary were always together when they lived on earth.

"Now Mary, the Mother of God, is in heaven with Him, too. She sees us all and loves us. It makes her very happy when we are good for love of Jesus. When little boys and girls have no mother on earth any more, then Mother Mary watches over them even more than over the other children. Sometimes children make the Mother of God feel sad. How can they do that? Suppose you have been naughty and have made Baby Jesus and His Mother Mary sad, what should you do? Tell them you are sorry and then Mary will smile at you again."

Teach the children a little prayer to the Blessed Virgin, short and simple; e.g., "Mary, with your Blessed Son, Bless us each and every one."

Review the hymns: "Baby Jesus Smiling" and "Mother Mary."

Madonna Booklet: Fold a half sheet of blue construction paper. Paste a pretty picture of Madonna and Child on the outside. Fasten white paper, folded as the blue, into the blue cover. Let the children write or copy from the board, short sentences such as: Mary and Jesus. I love Mary. I love Jesus. Mary is the Mother of Jesus. Jesus is God.

If there is time the teacher will read to the children parts of *Our Lord and Our Lady*, by Hilaire Belloc.

Remind the children often to make an Act of Contrition.

Pupil's Readings:

Rosary Primer, "Two Mothers," page 66.

American Primer, "Madonna," page 72.

Teacher's References:

Practical Aids, "The Blessed Virgin," Section VI.

Teacher's Notes:

The Wonderful Star
January, 2nd and 3rd Weeks; March, 3rd Week

Introduction:

Review: Where was the Baby Jesus born? Who is the Baby
Jesus? Who is His Mother? What did St. Joseph do for the little
Jesus? Who were the first people to visit the Infant Jesus? Did
the shepherds bring Jesus anything? Could they give Him much?
Did Jesus love them? What can you give the Baby Jesus?

Presentation:

"I am going to tell you about a beautiful star that God put
into the sky. It was the Baby Jesus' own star. God let it shine
so that the people would know that the Baby Jesus, His Son,
had come from heaven. Far, far away from Bethlehem there
lived three kings who were very wise and good. Every night they
used to watch the stars. One clear night they saw a new star in
the sky. It was brighter and more beautiful than any, of the
others. They said: 'Oh, look! There is a new star in the heavens.
How beautiful it is!' One of the kings said: 'That must be the
Little King's own star. Come let us go to find Him.' "

Review the story by showing the children the picture, *The
Star of the East,* by Doré. Let them retell the story.

Change the sand table so as to show the three kings on their
way over the desert; show an oasis; show the tents of the kings;
let the kings climb mountains and go through woods on their way
to Jerusalem.

Change again to show Jerusalem, or the hill country around
Bethlehem. Have the cave with crib in a prominent position.

Figures of kings, camels, servants, can be cut out and mounted
and be moved from day to day. Cut-outs may be purchased from
Co-op Parish Activities Service, Effingham, Ill.

"They took rich presents and rode away on camels to find the
Baby King. This Baby King was Jesus. They knew He was God.
The beautiful star shone very brightly and pointed out the way
to the three good kings."

Star Booklet: Children cut out a star on colored paper, silver or gold. Paste a picture of the Infant Jesus in the crib in the center. Cut out stars of similar size from white paper. Write these words: Jesus, Mary, Joseph, kings, star. Clasp papers as a booklet.

Pictures to Be Studied:

  The Star in the East — Doré.

  The Adoration of the Magi — Boticelli, Hofmann, Durer, Luini.

The Wise Men Find Jesus

Introduction:

Let the children read from *The Book of the Holy Child,* "The Wonderful Star," page 41, as far as "They followed the Star." Let them tell the story of the Wise Men on their journey in their own words.

Dramatize the scene of the star appearing to the Wise Men; they talk about it, get ready, and start their journey.

Presentation:

"Yes, the star showed the Wise Men the way to the Little King. But suddenly, when they came to Jerusalem, the star was gone. They went to the king, who lived in that city, and asked him: 'Where is the new-born King? We have seen His star and have come to adore Him.' Now this king Herod was a wicked man. He did not love God. He did not like to hear about a new king, because he was afraid he could not be king any more. He said to the three Wise Men: 'Go and find the Little King. When you have found Him, come and tell me where He is. I want to adore Him also.' In his heart, this wicked Herod thought: I will kill that new-born King."

Dramatize the scene before Herod; also at the Crib.

"When the Wise Men left the city, they looked up into the sky. There was their beautiful star again. They were so happy. They followed the star again. At last they came to Bethlehem. There the lovely star stood still, just above the poor little cave where Jesus was lying in the manger. The three kings were so happy. They climbed down from their big camels, took their rich presents of gold, incense, and myrrh, and went into the cave. The Baby Jesus knew they were coming. He smiled at them and held out His little arms to them. The three kings saw Jesus, their Little King, and 'falling down they adored Him' (Matt. ii. 11).

"They brought their beautiful gifts and gave them to their little God."

Study the picture, *Adoration of the Magi*, by Hofmann. Let the children retell the story often.

Dramatize Adoration of the Magi. See *Practical Aids*, page 242.

Creative Art: Cut or model a camel. Draw part of the story.

Robert Visits Jesus

Introduction:

Children read the story of "The Wonderful Star," *The Book of the Holy Child*, pages 42 to 44.

Presentation:

Let this lesson be one on Jesus in the Blessed Sacrament.

With intense love and devotion the teacher shall speak as her heart prompts her. The heart of the child must be drawn closer to the Heart of the Christ Child in the Blessed Sacrament from day to day. A few suggestions for this talk are:

Jesus loves you, His little child, more than anyone else.

Jesus wants you, His little child, to love Him, too.

Jesus lives in His golden house day and night because He wants you, His child, to visit Him.

Jesus is God and He will answer all your prayers.

Jesus wants to bless you and your parents, but you must ask Him to.

Jesus wants you to come to visit Him often.

Jesus wants your heart.

Soon Jesus will come into your heart in Holy Communion.

Jesus sees you all the time and when you pass the church always be polite to Him, by good conduct, by tipping your hat, by saying a prayer.

Children read "Robert Visits Jesus," pages 45–47.

During the singing class, teach the song "My Gift," by Rosetti.

End the lesson with the story, "Robert Visits Jesus," pages 45 to 47, and with a study of the picture on page 47.

The Return to the East

Introduction:

Sing or recite "My Gift," *The Book of the Holy Child,* page 48.

Study the picture on page 48.

Review:

Why did the Wise Men come to see little Jesus? Was Jesus glad to see them? Were Mother Mary and St. Joseph glad, too? What had the wicked King Herod told the Three Kings? What did He want to do with the Infant Jesus?

Presentation:

"The Wise Men did not know that the king in Jerusalem was a wicked man. Before they started back home, God sent an angel to them. The angel said: 'Do not go back to Herod. He wants to kill little Jesus.' They did not go back to Herod. The star showed them a new way home. King Herod was very angry. Are you glad that they went another way? King Herod tried to find Jesus to kill Him. He sent men to look for Jesus, but they could not find Him."

Read the lesson on page 49.

Poems and Quotations:

The teacher will read the following to the class:

"My Gift," Christina Rosetti; "In Church"; "Finding You," Marion Dixon Thayer; "And falling down, they adored Him."

Let the children often say the little prayer, "Jesus, teach me how to pray."

Pupil's Readings:

American First Reader, "The Wise Men," page 113; "The Story Father Told," pages 14–33.

Catholic Basic Primer, "New Home," page 136.

Corona First Reader, "The Wise Men and the Star," page 72.

Misericordia First Reader, "Little Star," page 38; "The Wise Men," pages 1–8.

Ideal Catholic Reader, I, "The Wise Men," page 50.

Teacher's References:

The Holy Bible, Gospel, St. Matthew, Chapter II.

Child's Garden of Religion Stories, "The Wise Men from the East," page 187.

Jesus of Nazareth, Mother Loyola, Chapter X, "The Star in the East."

Practical Aids, "The Adoration of the Magi, Dramatization," page 242; "Poster Design, the Magi," page 288; "The Wise Men at the Crib," page 99; "The Wise Men in Bethlehem," page 101; "The Wise Men Teach a Lesson," page 102.

The Little Ones, "The Story of the Wise Men," page 44; "The Blessed Sacrament," page 76.

To the Heart of the Child, "The Magi," pages 50–54.

Teacher's Notes:

UNIT VI

THE NATIVITY: POST-CHRISTMAS SEASON

The Visit of the Angel
January, 3rd and 4th Weeks; March, 4th Week

Introduction:

Review: Did the Wise Men return to King Herod? Why did this wicked king want to find Jesus Who told the Wise Men not to go back to Herod? How did they find their way home again? How did the wicked Herod feel when he found out that the three kings did not go back to him?

Presentation:

"One night after the Wise Men had left Bethlehem, God sent an angel to St. Joseph. St. Joseph was sleeping. Suddenly his room became as bright as day. St. Joseph in a dream saw God's angel. The angel said to St. Joseph: 'Arise, take the Child and His Mother and go into Egypt. Stay there until I tell you. Herod wants to kill the Child Jesus.' "

Study the picture of the "Angel's Visit to St. Joseph" in *The Book of Holy Child,* page 51; also the art picture, *Joseph's Dream,* by Crespi. Repeat the quotation, "Arise, take the child . . . ," in the review of the story of the picture, so that incidentally the children will learn it.

"At once Joseph woke up Mary and told her all the angel had said. They obeyed God. Soon they were on their way. Mother Mary with the Baby Jesus asleep in her arms, rode on the donkey. St. Joseph walked beside them and led the donkey. He took good care of them, always watching that Herod's wicked soldiers would not catch them."

Tell the legends of the Holy Child, if you wish. These are always interesting to the children: "The Child Jesus and the Leper Child"; "The Spider's Web"; "The Destruction of the Idols."

For these and similar legends, consult Luick's *Legends of the Child Jesus* (Benziger Bros.).

Show the picture, *Repose in Egypt*, by Plockhorst, or one of the following pictures and explain it to the children: *Joseph's Dream* and *Flight into Egypt*, in *The Book of the Holy Child*, pages 51 and 52; *Approaching the Home of Exile*, by Dastagnue; *Within the Shadows of the Pyramid*, by Giradet.

"They went on all night and for a number of days. They were very tired, but they kept right on. They knew God wanted it that way and that the angels were watching over them. They had God with them, for the little Baby Jesus was God. Nobody can really hurt you, when God is with you. God can do everything. He sees everything. He can look right into the hearts of people. He knows who is good and who is wicked. Let us tell Jesus we will always try to be good. Whisper to Jesus now: 'Dear Jesus, help me to be good. Dear Mother Mary, help me to keep my heart clean for Jesus.' "

Pictures That May Be Studied:
Flight into Egypt — Plockhorst.
Repose in Egypt — Plockhorst.

In Far-Away Egypt

Introduction:
Children read "Flight into Egypt," *The Book of the Holy Child*, page 51, and study the picture on page 52.

Presentation:
"When the Holy Family came to Egypt, they did not know anybody. St. Joseph had to look for work so he could buy food and clothing for Jesus and Mary. Do you know what kind of work St. Joseph did? Soon Baby Jesus learned to walk and talk. He would put His little arms around Mary and whisper to her, 'Mother!' When St. Joseph came home from work, little Jesus

would run to him and say, 'Dear St. Joseph!' How happy they all were. Later on when Jesus was about as old as you, He tried to help His Mother Mary work. Sometimes, too, St. Joseph would take Jesus to his workshop. Then Jesus tried to help St. Joseph, too. What do you think He could do? The picture on page 54, in your books, shows you. Now we shall read the lesson, 'In Far-Away Egypt.' Mother Mary told the people in Egypt about God. Are there any people now who do not know God?"

Here is a good opportunity to start the little children in foreign-mission work. Tell them about the thousands of heathen babies, who are exposed and thrown away, of the Sisters and Priests, who find them and baptize them, and teach them about God. Show them how they can help by offering their pennies at times; give them a mission box; tell them with five dollars the Priests and Sisters can buy these poor children and rear them as Catholics; that God will bless them if they help these missionaries. Mention prayers, too; perhaps even a little suggestion that sometime they might be Priests and Sisters like them, will not be out of place here. Show pictures of missions, the children, and the Priests and Sisters.

"Would you like to have been in Egypt to play with little Boy Jesus? Would you have been good to Him? That is the way Jesus wants you to treat all little girls and boys. Jesus says: 'When you are good to others, you are good to Me. And when you hurt others, you hurt Me.' Say to Jesus: 'Dear Jesus, I will not hurt them because it hurts You.'"

Encourage the children to tell the story at home to mother and father.

Teach a simple hymn to St. Joseph.

The Return Home
January, 4th Week; April, 1st Week

Introduction:

Show the children a beautiful picture of the Christ Child. Read the poem to the children, while they follow the words in their text, page 55.

Let them open their books to page 55, and read "Christ Our King." Have the children memorize it with thought and expression.

Presentation:

"Jesus grew stronger and bigger day by day in Egypt. Soon He was about six years old, just as old as you are. One night, when the Holy Family was asleep, the angel of God visited St. Joseph, the foster father of Jesus. The room of St. Joseph was suddenly filled with a bright light. There stood the same angel who had come to St. Joseph before."

Let the children tell the story of the angel's first visit to St. Joseph with the command to go to Egypt. Here the teacher might also tell the story of the massacre of the Holy Innocents; of their eternal reward in heaven.

"The angel said: 'Arise, take the Child and His Mother and go into the land of Israel. Those who wanted to kill Jesus are dead.' St. Joseph at once told Mother Mary the happy news that now they could go home, back to Nazareth. Joseph prepared to leave. Mary woke up Jesus and said to Him: 'Jesus, my God and my Darling Son, we are going home. Blessed be God!' Jesus smiled and was glad because His Mother was happy."

Dramatize the scene as follows:

[*Joseph is asleep; enter the angel.*]

ANGEL [*whispers softly*]: Joseph, Joseph.

JOSEPH: What do you want, dear angel?

ANGEL: God has sent me to you again. Arise, take the Child and His mother and go into the land of Israel. Those who wanted to kill Jesus are dead.

JOSEPH [*kneels down*]: My God, I obey.

ANGEL [*looks at Jesus and Mary asleep in the next room, kneels down, prays*]: Jesus, my God, I adore You [*then quietly leaves*].

JOSEPH [*going to Mary*]: Mary, sweet Mary, the angel of God has been here. We must go back home to Nazareth.

MARY [*kneels a moment*]: My God, I obey You. [*Awakens Jesus*] Jesus, my little Boy, wake up. God calls us home to Nazareth.

JESUS [*rubbing His eyes and smiling*]: Yes, dear Mother, I obey.

Develop this dramatization as far as desired. Angels hover near, praying, watching over them, accompanying them on their departure.

Talk about their home journey through the desert, their suffering, how they slept on the sand with only a blanket for protection, how the angels hovered about them.

Now read the lesson, "The Return Home," pages 56, 57.

The Hardships of Jesus

Introduction:

Review the hardships which Jesus had to suffer in His short life of about six years. The inconveniences of Bethlehem, the hatred of Herod and the flight into Egypt, their long stay in Egypt, finally their first day and night on the return trip. Again show the children the pictures used in this plan to correspond with the above scenes. While so doing, draw attention to the sufferings of the Child Jesus and Mary and St. Joseph.

Presentation:

"Jesus, Mary, and Joseph were so poor! Think of it, Jesus was God. He had made everything and everything was His. Why did He want to suffer like this? Jesus is your little Leader. He knew His little children would have to suffer sometimes, for He would send them little sorrows. Jesus suffered because He loved you. He sends you little pains and sorrows because He wants you to show Him that you love Him. What must children like you suffer sometimes? (Let them suggest.) What a brave little child you can be. Jesus will love you, oh, so much, when you say to Him, 'Jesus, I will suffer this headache for You.' But most little children do not get sick. They can show Jesus in many other ways that they love Him. They can do something hard for Him like getting up early to come to Mass. They can save their pennies for the little heathen babies."

Discussion with the children of little acts of self-denial they can offer to Jesus. Let these be suitable to their age, acts of silence in school; charity to one of their friends especially to a poor child; standing and sitting straight; mortification by eating something they do not like so well.

"Children, when you come to heaven some day, Jesus will take you into His arms. He will press you tight against His Heart and say: 'I loved you most, My little child, when you suffered for Me.' Won't you be happy now, to offer Jesus a little bit of suffering every day?"

Home in Nazareth

Introduction:

A song to Jesus; one to Mary; one to St. Joseph — one stanza of each.

The aspiration, "Jesus, Mary, Joseph, I give you my heart and my soul."

Presentation:

"Jesus, Mary, and Joseph were nearing home. The journey was almost over. They had left Egypt a few days ago, had walked through the desert, up hills, through villages, and cities. They were very, very tired, but so happy. God had told them to return to Nazareth and they obeyed Him. That is why they were so happy. Now they are on the hill near Nazareth. St. Joseph holds Jesus in his arms and says to Him: 'Dear Jesus, see that little town at the bottom of the hill. That is Nazareth. Dear Mary, there is Home!' They all walk down the hill quickly, and dear little Jesus sees His home for the first time. Soon they are in their home. The Blessed Mother says: 'Let us thank God.' And Jesus, Mary, and Joseph kneel down and thank God for bringing them home."

Read, "The Return Home," *The Book of the Holy Child,* page 56.

Dramatize the home-coming of the Holy Family.

Have the children use the ejaculation "Blessed be God" in this dramatization.

Let the children arrange the sand table to illustrate the return journey, step by step.

Have them make posters of a desert scene with obelisk, sphinx, oasis, a few wild animals.

UNIT VII

THE CHILDHOOD OF JESUS

At Home: Christ's Love for His Parents
April, 2nd Week

Introduction:

Song: "Mary, Mother of God."

Read the Lesson, "Honor Thy Father and Thy Mother," page 58.

Presentation:

"Jesus, Mary, and Joseph were now home after their long journey through the desert. God wanted them to live in Nazareth. They were so happy to be safe at home. St. Joseph was the father of the little home; dear Mary was the mother; and Jesus, the God of heaven and earth, was the little Child in the family."

Study the picture of the Holy Family, stressing in this study the love of the members for each other. Always refer to the child's own family when possible.

"Jesus loved His Mother Mary and His foster father, St. Joseph. He loved them because it was God's will. He loved them also because they were so holy, and because they took such good care of Him. When you were a little child, God gave you to your parents, to father and mother. God wants you to love your parents more than anybody else on earth. You must love them because God commands you to love them. God made you for heaven; you are God's little child. God gave you to mother and father because He knew they would take good care of you. How much God loves you to give you to such good parents. Whisper to God in your heart: 'Thank You, dear God, for giving me such good parents.'"

Continue to develop the thought of love for parents. Keep constantly before the minds of the children that their parents take God's place; that they must love their parents because God commands them to. Only secondary, but nevertheless very important, is the thought that they love their parents because they are so good to them, take care of them in sickness, provide food, clothing, shelter for them. All these thoughts should be discussed with the children.

Pictures That May Be Studied:

The Holy Family — Ittenbach, Murillo.
Jesus in the Workshop — Hofmann.

The Happy Helpers: Obedience
April, 2nd Week

Introduction:

The teacher will read or recite the "Disobedient Robin" by Phoebe Cary.

Ask the children to repeat the story.

Presentation:

"Once upon a time God said to all the children in the world: 'Honor thy father and thy mother' (Exod. xx. 12). Jesus loved His parents; Jesus is your Leader. He will love and reward you if you honor your parents. Children, God will punish you if you do not honor your father and mother. You want to do just what Jesus did. He loved and obeyed His parents because God wanted Him to. You, too, like your little Leader Jesus, must love and obey your parents because God said so. You honor and love your parents if you obey them."

Discuss with the children many little problems of obedience that actually occur in the home. Let the children give occasions on which they have been happy because they obeyed mother and father. For typical problems, see *Teaching the Ten Commandments*, "The Fourth Commandment," pages 72–92. However, only those problems, which refer to children of this age, should be discussed.

Let the children tell how they can help mother and father in the home.

Develop each of the following points:

a) Our parents take the place of God.

b) We must obey parents because God commands it.

c) The best way to show our love to parents is through obedience, willing, cheerful, prompt.

d) We must never make our parents sad by naughty actions, at home, in the street, in school.

e) Help mother and father wherever we can.

f) God gave all our brothers and sisters to our parents.

g) Make father and mother happy and proud of us by always being a little lady or gentleman; by studying well at school; by behaving all the time.

h) Gods wants us to pray for our parents every day.

"Kneel down, children and let us say a Hail Mary for our parents. Say, 'God, bless my father and my mother.'"

Let the children now open *The Book of the Holy Child*. Read and then pray the "Little Offering," on page 59. Tell the children to say this prayer every day so that Jesus will help them to obey.

Pupil's Readings:

American Reader I, "The Holy Family," page 42; "I Wanted a Brother," page 97.

Ideal Catholic Reader, I, "Papa and Mama," page 89.

Teacher's References:

The Holy Bible, Exodus xx. 12.

First Communion, Chapter X, "Nazareth," page 113.

Jesus of Nazareth, Chapter XI, "Jesus of Nazareth," page 85.

Teacher Tells a Story, Vol. II, "Stories on Obedience," pages 109–141.

Teaching the Ten Commandments, "The Fourth Commandment," pages 72–92.

Practical Aids, "The Boy Jesus at Home," page 106; "The Example of Jesus," page 106.

Teacher's Notes:

Christ's Love of Home
April, 2nd Week

Introduction:

Recite the poem, "The Little Offering," *The Book of the Holy Child,* page 59.

Read "At Home," page 61.

Let the children talk about the picture of the Holy Family in *The Book of the Holy Child,* page 61.

Sand-Table Project: Arrange the sand table to represent the hill country of Nazareth. Build the home of the Holy Family in the valley, a little removed from the other houses. Show the rooms described in their imaginary visit; let the children arrange the scene as they wish. An outside scene could be arranged, with a well, a flower garden, a path leading to the house, Joseph's workshop at a distance away. See *Practical Aids,* page 232.

Presentation:

"Jesus, Mary, and Joseph were the happiest people on earth. They lived in a poor little house in Nazareth. They loved each other, they helped each other. Jesus helped St. Joseph. He helped His dear Mother Mary. How did Jesus help them?"

Talk about the little home duties that Jesus performed. Tell the children how He did all this for love of God and parents and to show all children how to live happily.

"Would you like to see where Jesus lived? It was a little house, perhaps like the one in this picture."

Show the picture of *Jesus Getting Water,* in *Wonder Days.* Talk about the picture.

An imaginary visit to Nazareth: If desired, let this take place as described below, or the teacher can herself just give a description of the probable home of Jesus.

"Let us think we are in Nazareth. Now we will open the front door of Jesus' house, but oh, so quietly, because this is God's house. How poor it is! See, here is the rough table where the Holy Family eat their meals. In this cupboard, Mother Mary puts the dishes. Whose are the little cup and plate? This clean wooden box is for Jesus' clothes. Oh, look in this corner, all the little wooden toys! Whose are they? Who made them? Some blocks, a little lamb, a few clay birds, a sprinkling can, and oh! look at this, a wooden cross! Who made that do you think? Jesus loved us so much. When He grew up to be a Man, He died for love of us on a big wooden cross. Let us make the Sign of the Cross now to show Jesus we love Him."

Continue the above, imagining you are in the bedroom of Jesus, in the kitchen, in Joseph's workshop.

"Jesus is the God of heaven and earth. He could have had the most beautiful home on earth. Why did He live in this poor house? Why did Mary and Joseph love this poor house? Just think, Jesus came down from His golden heaven and lived in such a poor house because He loved us."

Talk to the children about their own homes, their good father and mother, how they can help to keep their homes happy and clean. End by saying:

"Often say to Jesus, 'Thank You, dear God, for my home, for my good father and mother. My home and Jesus' home are holy places.' "

Booklet: "Jesus' Home and My Home." Let the children paste pictures of the home of Jesus (holy cards), and any picture to illustrate their own home. Also a picture of a Catholic church would be suitable. Let them write short sentences such as: This is Jesus' home. Jesus lives in church. This is my home. My home and Jesus' home are holy. Pictures of St. Joseph, Mary, their own parents. Write short sentences beneath each.

Orderliness and Cleanliness
April, 2nd Week

Introduction:
Review briefly the appearance of Jesus' home.
Presentation:
"Jesus helped St. Joseph to keep his shop in good order. He picked up the little bits of wood and shavings. When He got a little older, He helped St. Joseph at his work. When He was at

home with His dear Mother, He helped to keep the house clean. You see, children, Jesus wanted to teach all His little children to act the way He did in all things. You, too, must help your parents to keep your homes clean."

Read the lesson, "At Home," page 61, *The Book of the Holy Child.*

Discuss the little things children of their age can do to keep the home tidy; also the school.

"Jesus loves to see you, His little child, clean, too. But most of all He wants to see your heart clean, just as clean as His golden home on the altar. How can you keep your heart clean? Jesus lives in every little child's heart, if it is clean and pure. Whisper something beautiful to Jesus in your heart. Say: 'O sweet Jesus, help me to keep my heart clean for You.' Jesus also wants to see your body clean."

Discuss with the children the simple rules of cleanliness. Let each one be centered around the thought, "Jesus lives in my soul. He wants to see my body and soul clean."

Make posters on cleanliness, orderliness. Cut pictures from advertisements in magazines and arrange as suitable health posters.

Love of Nature
April, 2nd Week

Introduction:

Show the picture *Jesus Watering the Flowers,* in *The Wonder Days.* What do you see in this picture? Who made the pretty flowers? What is Jesus doing? Who planted these flowers? To whom did Jesus give some flowers? Who has a flowerbed at home?

Let them tell about their flowers, how they care for them. Tell them that God sends the sunshine, the rain, to make the flowers grow for them.

Presentation:

"Jesus lives in His little golden house on the altar all the time. If you wish to give Him some flowers, bring them to Sister. She will give Him the flowers and He will bless and love you. To whom else can you give your flowers? (To Mary the mother of Jesus, to my own mother, to the sick.)

"Your prayers are like beautiful flowers. You can offer to Jesus a pretty flower when you say a little prayer to Him. Let us give Jesus a beautiful rose now. Whisper to Him: 'Jesus, I love You.'"

Teach the poem, "The Child Jesus," page 62, as a prayer.

"You can give Jesus some sweet fruit, too. You do this by little acts of kindness, of obedience, of politeness. Tell mother and father tonight about the flowers and fruit you gave Jesus today. Ask them to give Jesus some, too."

Any picture of Jesus in some connection with Nature.

Class Project: Teacher suggests a flower illustrative of the respective virtue to be practiced for the day. Draw or paste a flower on the board and call attention to it during the day; e.g., rose — do an act of kindness; lily — say a prayer to the Blessed Virgin.

Pupil's Readings:

American First Reader, "The Garden," page 119.

Catholic Child, I, "The Home of Jesus," page 1; "St. Francis and the Birds," page 53.

Corona, I, "Beautiful World," page 70; "Home in Nazareth," page 86.

Teacher's References:

Practical Aids, "Orderliness," pages 49–53; "Cleanliness," pages 66–69; "Jesus' Love for Pure Hearts," page 92; "Jesus' Love for Kind Hearts," page 92; "Sand-Table Project," page 232.

The Little Ones, "Short Informal Talks"; page 48; "Jesus At Home"; "Our Lord and Our Lady at Home"; "The Workshop"; and "Our Lady's Love of Flowers," page 48.

Teacher's Notes:

The Work of Jesus
April, 3rd Week

Introduction:

Review: Whom did Jesus love most on this earth? What could Jesus do to show them His love? Jesus helped His dear Mother Mary and His foster father St. Joseph whenever He could.

Teacher will read the poem, "Nazareth," by Father Doyle, to the children. Study this poem.

During the course of the week, have them memorize it.

Presentation:

"In the morning the dear Mother of Jesus worked about the house just as your own good mother does. What did she do? What could little Jesus do to help His sweet Mother? How can you help your mother? When you help mother, try to think that once upon a time, Jesus, your little Leader, did just what you are doing. Often say to Him, 'Jesus, I will do this work for love of You.'

"When Jesus was strong enough to work harder, He went with St. Joseph to their little shop. St. Joseph was a carpenter."

Talk over with the children the work a carpenter does, the things he makes and mends. Keep before them the thought that St. Joseph and Jesus did just that kind of work. Construct St. Joseph's workshop on the sand table.

"St. Joseph did all this rough work. Jesus, who knew how to do all things, wanted St. Joseph to teach Him. After their breakfast Jesus and St. Joseph said good-by to Mother Mary and started off for the workshop. Jesus often looked back and waved His hand to His dear Mother. When they came to the shop, they began to work at once. How do you think Jesus could help St. Joseph? How can you help your father?"

Show and discuss the picture of Jesus in the workshop.

"When Jesus obeyed and helped His parents, He always smiled and was happy. Sometimes Jesus was tired from all the work, but He never grumbled. Oh, no! When you help mother and father, and always are happy to work for them, Jesus loves you. He smiles on you and blesses you. But when you run away and do not want to do what mother or father tells you to do, Jesus is sad. Dear children, when you are happy and work with a smile, everybody loves you, mother and father, Sister in school, and your guardian angel. But most of all does God love His little child. Surely, you all want to follow your little Leader, Jesus, and always do what He wants you to do, especially to obey your dear mother and father."

Read, "The Happy Helpers," page 63.

Make a booklet on Obedience. Paste in it pictures of Jesus, parents (any pictures of man and woman cut from magazines), Sister, others in authority, and write sentences like the following:

I obey Jesus.

Honor thy father and thy mother.

I obey Sister.

God wants me to obey my parents.

Find picture of children at work in the home, in the garden, running errands. Make a poster of each or paste in the above booklet and write short sentences.

Show the children the picture, *Christ Helping His Mother*, in *The Wonder Days*. Study it with them.

Pictures That May Be Studied:

Christ in the Workshop — Hofmann.

Christ in the Workshop — Taggart (in *The Wonder Days*).

Teacher's References:

Practical Aids, "Work," page 45; "We All Must Work," page 46; "Learn to Like Your Work," page 47; "The Blessing of Work," page 48; "Cheerfulness," pages 5–17.

The Little Ones, "The Workshop of St. Joseph," page 48; "St. Joseph's Work as a Carpenter," page 85.

Teacher Tells a Story, Vol. II, "Stories on Obedience," pages 109–141.

Teacher's Notes:

Play, Gentleness, and Courtesy of Jesus
April, 3rd Week

Introduction:

Let the children tell all they can about the pictures on pages 60 and 65, "The Little Teacher," in *The Book of the Holy Child*. Have them select one of the children they would like to be. Each one will tell the class what he is doing and saying to Jesus, and what Jesus is doing and saying to him. Note especially the gentleness of Jesus and His courtesy to the children.

Presentation:

"Jesus often asked His little friends of Nazareth to come to His home. Sometimes He played games or walked with them. Sometimes He taught them, as you see in this picture."

Discuss with the children various pictures of Jesus in His play. Mount these pictures and at times let the children describe them to the class and tell the lesson Jesus teaches them through this picture. Enjoy the following pictures with the children:

Divine Shepherd — Murillo.

Children of the Shell — Murillo.

The Christ Child — Ittenbach.

Jesus Watering Flowers (in *The Wonder Days*).

Christ and St. John the Baptist — Azambre.

A Little Child Shall Lead Them — Strut.

"Let us go to Jesus' home and play with Him, too (imaginary trip to Jesus' home). Here is the path leading up to Jesus' home. A dear, sweet lady is at the door. She is Mary, the Mother of Jesus. Listen to what Mary says: 'Good morning, dear children. Jesus! Come, here are some dear little children. They want to play with You.' A sweet, beautiful Boy comes to the door. Jesus holds out His arms to us and, smiling, says: 'Come, My little friends. Mother, may I play with these boys and girls?' Mother Mary says to Him: 'Yes, my dear Boy, play as long as You like.' Jesus says (mention different children in the class): 'Joseph, Charlotte, help Me carry My toys outside.' We shall go into Jesus' house and help Him bring out His toys. (Describe the toys and the play of the children vividly.)

Read and discuss with the children *The Birds*, by Hilaire Belloc.

"Now a game of tag! Jesus is It. Oh, He is running after me! Yes, Jesus has caught me. Oh, dear Jesus, hold me tight, I always want to be close to You."

Ball Game

"Jesus has the ball. One little girl is standing all alone. Jesus throws the ball to her. How happy she is because Jesus plays with her.

"Oh, how fast the time has gone. We have played two hours with Jesus. Now the sweet Mother comes again to the door, she calls: 'Jesus, come to me.' Jesus runs to His Mother. Oh, how good Jesus and Mary are. Here they come out of the house with some milk and bread for all of us. Jesus and Mother Mary wait on us poor little children. Jesus is the great God of Heaven and earth, and Mother Mary is the holy Mother of God. How much they love us! Now once more dear Mary says: 'Children, your mothers are waiting for you. It is time to go home. Come again to play with Jesus!' We all say: 'Good-by, dear Jesus. Thank you, dear Mother,' and here we are back home in the classroom.

"Do you play with other children just as Jesus did?"

Here is a good opportunity to develop the attitude of fair play, unselfishness in games, peaceableness. The teacher should correct what she has noticed in the children's play necessary of correction.

Courtesy

Presentation:

"Jesus is your little Leader in everything. How sweet and polite He always was. In the morning when He woke up, He was polite to God by saying His prayers. Then He ran to His sweet Mother Mary, put His arms around her and said: 'Good morning, Mother,' and also to St. Joseph."

Speak of the courtesy of Jesus all through the day toward His parents, toward strangers, visitors, friends, old people until His last act of courtesy at night. Jesus is their Model, is the thought to be kept in mind throughout these discussions.

Dramatization: Teach the children little politeness rules toward their parents. Dramatize scenes of home life in which the following and similar expressions of courtesy are used: Good Morning; thank you, Father; I am sorry, Mother; please forgive me; I love you; please, may I have this? Teach the boys to take off their hats when meeting their mothers, teachers, older people on the street.

Similarly scenes of courtesy on the street, in the school, in church can be simply dramatized and in this way easily learned.

Discuss courtesy in school (*Practical Aids*, pages 20–22), on the street, and on the playgrounds. As the teacher notices the failings of the children on these points, she should correct them. Certainly not all the rules of courtesy ought to be taken during the religion class. However, a few, especially those which refer to parents, teachers, priests, old people, should be taken so as to instill in the hearts of the children a reverent, religious attitude toward their superiors. Always emphasize the fact that Jesus did it so, and Jesus is their Leader.

Posters on courtesy can be made by the children and exhibited in the classroom.

The Little Teacher: Kindness, Good Companionship
April, 4th Week

Introduction:

"Once upon a time a blind man went out walking. He could not see the beautiful sky, the bright sun, the pretty birds and flowers. He walked through a meadow. Suddenly he smelt the sweetest flower. Remember he could not see it. He walked about and finally reached the little flower.

"Are you the beautiful rose I have been smelling?" he asked the flower.

"No," said the little flower. "I am only a tiny little white flower."

"But you smell just like a rose," said the blind man.

"Oh," answered the flower, "You see, sir, I have lived so close to a lovely rose, which somebody plucked this morning, that I, too, smell like the rose."

Presentation:

"Children, the most beautiful rose that ever grew can never be so sweet as a good little child. Jesus was the best little Child that ever lived. He was the sweetest Rose God ever made. If boys and girls would stay near Jesus all day long, they would soon be like Him, they would smell as sweet as the little white flower. You can all stay near Jesus by often praying to Him, by thinking of Him, by obeying, and working for Him. Then, too, you can be near Jesus in another lovely way, that is, by having only good little children as your friends. All the children, who came to see Jesus, were sweet, pure children, and oh, how much Jesus loved them."

Now speak to the children on the virtues they must strive to acquire and which those children with whom they play should possess; also of the vices they must conquer.

Truthfulness, *Practical Aids*, pages 54–57.

Honesty, *Practical Aids*, pages 58–59.

Gentleness, *Practical Aids*, pages 5–17.

Purity in talk and action.

Stealing, *Practical Aids*, pages 59–61.

Obedience.

Discuss the above topics with the children only insofar as their age and necessity require. Dwell especially upon the virtues, not the vices. Make very clear that only good children should be their companions.

Pictures:

The Little Teacher, in *The Book of the Holy Child*, page 65.
Children of the Shell — Murillo.

The Children of the Shell
April, 4th Week

Introduction:

Study the picture on page 66, *The Book of the Holy Child;* then also Murillo's *Children of the Shell.*

Read the lesson on page 66.

Presentation:

Speak of Jesus' kindness to Mary and Joseph; to His little friends; to the flowers and animals; to the poor, the sick, and the old.

"Jesus has been most kind to you. Can you tell me what Jesus has done for you?"

Discuss the kindness of God shown to them by giving them good parents, home, sunshine, flowers, little pets, friends, guardian angel; because God made them for heaven.

"The best present Jesus has given to you, His little children, is Himself. Jesus lives in His little golden house in church just for you. Soon Jesus will come from that little house of His to you. The priest will put Jesus on your tongue and Jesus will really be in your hearts. Oh, how good Jesus is to you!"

Read and memorize "A Prayer," page 67, *The Book of the Holy Child.*

"My Friends" Booklet: Let the children cut out pictures from religious magazines and others of Jesus, Mary, Joseph, patron saints, grandma, baby, animals, flowers, etc.

Write a short sentence beneath each, as the children wish.

Jesus is my best friend.

Mother and Father are my best friends on earth.

Teacher's References:

Practical Aids, "Politeness," pages 18–34.

The Little Ones, "Informal Talks, Our Lord Played," page 49.

Teacher's Notes:

The Study of Jesus
April, 4th Week

Introduction:

"Jesus, Mary's Son and the Son of God, has said 'Learn of Me.' When the little boys and girls came to Jesus, what did He teach them? Why did Jesus love these children? How did they make Jesus happy? How can you make Jesus happy?"

Read again "The Little Teacher," page 65.

Presentation:

"Jesus was a little child just like you. He loved to play and run about. Jesus studied His lessons, too, just as all good children do."

Study the picture, *Mary and Her Divine Son*, by Jannson, and the following if they are available: *Jesus At Study* (in *The Wonder Days*), and *He Was Subject to Them*, by Winter.

"Jesus is God. He knows all things. When He was a little Boy, He knew everything. Jesus did not have to study. He wanted to be your Leader in all things. He wanted to show you how to study. Jesus went to school, too. Mary, His dear Mother, and St. Joseph, His foster father, were His teachers. Sometimes Jesus had to recite His lessons to the priests in the synagogue. Many other little boys were there, too. Jesus often helped a poor little boy with his lessons. He will help you, too, if you ask Him. Often whisper to Jesus, 'Dear Jesus, bless my studies! Bless my work! All for You, dear Jesus!' If your lessons are a little hard, say quietly to Jesus: 'Jesus, I will do my best for You, no matter how hard it is.' How much Jesus will love you. He will smile at you from heaven and bless you."

Develop the following points (always keep before the minds of the children that Jesus is their Leader and that He wants them to act just as He did in all situations):

a) God wants them to study, so as to know Him better, to become more like Jesus every day.

b) If children are good and try their best, Jesus will bless their studies.

c) They must behave in school as Jesus did. Jesus sees them all the time.

d) They must behave as little ladies and gentlemen: on the way to and from school; in the school; on the playground for love of Jesus.

e) Jesus will love them if they help good children who cannot get their lessons.

f) They must love and obey their teachers because God has given them charge of the children in the name of parents.

Dramatize the simple school courtesies toward teachers; make posters on this topic.

Read "At Study," *The Book of the Holy Child*, page 69. Discuss the pictures.

Teacher's Notes:

Jesus at Prayer
May, 1st Week

Introduction:

Let the children read the lesson in *The Book of the Holy Child*, "Jesus at Prayer," page 70, as an introduction to the study of prayer.

Study the picture of *Christ at Prayer*, in *The Book of the Holy Child*, page 70.

Show a picture of *Herman Joseph at Prayer*, and tell the children the story.

Show the picture of *St. Mary the Virgin*, by Ittenbach. Mount these and similar pictures and during the weeks of study on prayer, let the children have continual access to them. Display them in the classroom.

Teach the poem or the song, "Jesus Teach Me How to Pray." Let them sing or recite it often during the course of this study.

Presentation:

"Dear children, Jesus wants you to pray often to Him, and to His Father in heaven. He will always listen to you, if you think of Him when you pray. He wants you to pray to His dear mother, too. I'm going to tell you a story about a little boy who loved to pray to Jesus and Mary.

"Once upon a time, a long, long time ago, there lived a poor little boy. His name was Herman Joseph. Little Herman was a very good boy. He loved the Baby Jesus and Baby Jesus loved him. Mother Mary, Jesus' sweet mother, loved Herman Joseph, too. Little Herman often went to visit Baby Jesus and Mother Mary in church and to pray. Oh, he loved so much to pray to Jesus and Mary. He always knelt before the altar and thought only of Jesus and Mary.

"One day in the cold, cold winter, poor little Herman Joseph was on his way to church, barefooted. Through the biting cold snow he walked and slowly came near the church. His feet were all swollen with the cold and so he could not go quickly. Suddenly, a most beautiful lady, dressed in a long white dress and a lovely blue veil, stood before him. He stopped.

" 'Dear little Herman Joseph,' said the sweet lady. 'Why are you barefooted in this cold weather.'

" 'Oh, dear Lady,' he answered her, 'because my parents are too poor to buy me shoes and stockings.'

"Then the lady pointed to a large stone and said to him: 'Lift up that stone, my boy.'

"Herman Joseph obeyed the lady and there he found enough money to buy shoes and stockings.

"He knew that the lady was the Mother of Jesus. He knelt down before her and thanked her. Dear Mother Mary smiled at him and disappeared.

"The Blessed Virgin and Baby Jesus rewarded little Herman

because he loved them and often prayed to them. Jesus and Mary will love you also if you pray. They will reward you, too, and bless you every day."

Teach the poem or the song, "Jesus Teach Me How to Pray." Let them sing or recite it often during the course of this study.

Morning Prayer

Introduction:

Sing or recite the poem, "Jesus Teach Me How to Pray."

Presentation:

"Jesus loved to pray! As soon as He opened His eyes in the morning from His night's sleep, He thought of God in heaven, His Father. Kneeling, He folded His little hands, and said, 'My Father in heaven, I love You.' Then He spoke to God a little longer. He prayed for His dear mother, for St. Joseph, and for you. How much Jesus loved you. He thought of you all the time. After Jesus had finished His morning prayer, He quickly ran over to His dear mother and said: 'Good morning, dear Mother.' Then He put His little arms about her and told her again and again that He loved her.

"Jesus is your Leader. He wants you to pray just as He did. What prayer did you say this morning when you woke up?"

Let different ones recite their morning prayer, teach a short morning prayer to those who do not know any. Suggest to them the good intention by saying: "All for Thee, dear Jesus"; also review the Our Father and the Hail Mary, the Guardian Angel Prayer carefully.

"God wants to hear your prayer every morning. He will feel sad if His little child does not even think of Him. God takes good care of you all night. He protects you during the night. What should you say to God for all this kindness? God takes care of mother, father, brother, and sister all night, too. See how much God loves you. Ask God every morning to bless mother and father and all the family. Promise Him that you will be a good child all day."

Have the children read "Morning Prayer," *The Book of the*

Holy Child, page 71, and memorize the last five lines of it. Encourage them to say these lines as soon as they awaken. The very first act of the day should be the Sign of the Cross with the prayer, "All for Thee, O Jesus."

"After Jesus had said His morning prayer and good morning to Mother Mary and to St. Joseph, He helped His mother set the table for breakfast. Then He folded His hands again and with His mother and St. Joseph asked God to bless their meal. During the meal He was very polite. Jesus wants you to be just like Himself."

Let the children recite the prayer which they say at home before and after meals. Teach those, who do not know any, a short prayer. Tell them to ask father and mother to say this prayer aloud at meals.

Here could be taught a few acts of courtesy at meals toward parents and others present. Always place Jesus before them as their model. Virtues that can be practiced at meal time should be discussed; e.g., acts of mortification, of obedience, of gentleness, self-control.

"When the meal was over, the Holy Family thanked God in heaven for His goodness toward them. What does Jesus want you to do after your meals?"

Pictures That May Be Studied:
The Child Samuel — Reynolds.
St. Mary, the Virgin — Ittenbach.
Jesus at Prayer (in *The Wonder Days*).

Pupil's Readings:
Catholic Child, I, "Manners," page 80; "Child's Prayer," page 82; "The Lord's Prayer," page 121.

Corona, I, "A Child's Prayer," Tabb, page 64; "Morning Prayer," R. Benson, page 71.

Ideal Catholic Reader, I, "Samuel at Prayer," page 27.

Rosary Primer, "Good Morning," pages 6–19; "Breakfast," pages 20–33.

Teacher's References:
Practical Aids.

Teacher Tells a Story, Vol. II, pages 193–196; "Prayer," pages 199–203.

Teacher's Notes:

Early Prayer
May, 1st and 2nd Weeks

Introduction:

The teacher will read to the class the poem, "Early Prayer," by M. D. Thayer, in *The Book of the Holy Child,* page 72. The children follow her in their books.

Presentation:

"Jesus was a little child just like you. All day long He was happy and He made others happy. He loved to help His mother, Mary and His foster father, St. Joseph. When He was old enough, He loved to study. What Jesus loved to do best of all was to pray. He often prayed during the day. He folded His little hands and looked up to heaven. God, the Father in heaven, watched His dear Son Jesus, and smiled at Him. Do you often say a little prayer to God during the day?"

Teach the children to say ejaculations often during the day:

"All for Thee, O Jesus."

"Dear God, I love You."

"Blessed Be God."

"Jesus, Mary, Joseph, I give You my heart and my soul."

At times during the day let the children say one of these aloud.

"You are God's little child. God made you to know Him, to love Him, and some day to be in heaven with Him. You love mother and father very, very much, but you must love God the

best. Say in your heart, 'My God, Jesus, I love You, I love You
best of all.' How can you show God you love Him?" Let the
children suggest various ways.

"There is still another way you can show Jesus that you love
Him. Your mother and father love you very much. They often
think of their little child. You can show God you love Him by
often thinking of Him. When you walk to school, you can say
to Jesus, 'Jesus, walk with me to school.' When you see a pretty
flower, you can say, 'Jesus, You made the pretty flower for me,
thank You.'"

Talk about any number of actual situations in the child's life
that can remind him of the presence of God.

Study the picture, *Omnipresence of God,* by Hofmann.

Try to get the children to realize according to their capacity,
that God is present all the time, sees and hears all they do, say,
or think. He will reward them for all the good they do, and
punish them for all the naughty things they do.

Make a collection and mount all pictures which deal in any
way with prayer such as:

Jesus at Prayer — Marion Taggart (in *The Wonder Days*).

Jesus and St. John — Reni.

The Virgin — Ittenbach.

The Consoling Christ — Plockhorst.

Repose in Egypt — Plockhorst.

Christ Blessing Little Children — Hofmann.

Worship of the Wise Men — Hofmann.

The Last Supper — Hofmann.

Prayer — G. Max.

Samuel at Prayer — Reynolds.

Prodigal Son — Molitor.

Angels in Adoration.

Children at Prayer.

Read to the children the poem, "Thoughts," from *The Child
on His Knees,* by Thayer, page 85. Children repeat the ideas
expressed in the poem and, if possible, memorize it. Also read
and explain the simpler parts of *Little Jesus,* by Francis
Thompson.

"Jesus' study, work, and play were prayers, because He did all for God. No matter what you do, always say to Jesus: 'Jesus, I will study for You. Jesus, I will play for You. Jesus, I will work for You. Jesus, I will obey mother for You.' If you do that, all your study, work, and play will be a prayer to Jesus. He will love and bless you."

Teach the poems, "At Play," page 83; "For You," page 78; "I Love You," page 48, *The Child on His Knees,* by M. D. Thayer.

Let the children read them again and again during the course of the week. Reward those who have them memorized.

"Jesus loved to go to the house of God. It was like our church, but the Jews called it a synagogue. Jesus went to the synagogue with His parents very, very often. He wanted to pray in God's house for everybody. He prayed for all the little children. Jesus prayed for you. How much Jesus loves you. Jesus lives in His little golden house on the altar in church for you. He is always waiting for you. He wants you to come to Him every day. He looks for you from His golden home and He is so happy when He sees His little child come to Him. He sees you and He listens to your prayers.

"When you are in church, just look at Jesus all the time. He is smiling at you. Tell Jesus how much you love Him. Say all the little prayers and poems and songs you know."

Review the poems and prayers the children have studied during the year. Encourage them to say these prayers and poems to Jesus in church. The words of the hymns can be said as prayers.

"All little boys and girls who are seven years old, must go to Mass every Sunday. If you do not go, you make God very, very sad. It is a big sin, if you miss Mass on Sundays. Mother and father must go to Mass, too, on Sundays. They will tell you when it is time to go to church. When you are sick, Mother will tell you to stay home. God wants you to obey mother. Then you must stay at home and God will not be sad. You can say your prayers at home and God will love you."

Speak to the children on attendance at Mass and at various devotions. However, little children should not be expected too frequently in church. Tell them to ask their parents to take them to church sometimes.

The two poems, "In Church," and "Perhaps He Won't," by Thayer, pages 12 and 42, can be given as supplementary reading. Let a few of the children who read well, read them to the class.

Repeat the various parts of the lesson while engaging in the following added activities:

a) Set up the synagogue or a church on the sand table; cut out pictures of children and adults, mount and show them on the way to church. If the synagogue is used, let these pictures be of Jesus, Mary, Joseph, Jewish boys and girls.

b) Take the class to the church; after an act of adoration, show them the various objects in the church and tell them their use.

c) Let the children cut from religious catalogs pictures of objects used in the church. Let each child tell to the class for what it is used.

d) Have the children read or the teacher read to the children the poems, "In the Morning," "To Our Lady," "Thanksgiving," from *The Child On His Knees*.

Pupil's Readings:

Catholic Child, "Night and Day," page 120.

Corona, I, "Mary's Altar," page 117; "I Pray to God," page 25.

Ideal Catholic Reader, I, "Love of Jesus," page 12; "Behavior at Mass," page 76.

Rosary Primer, "The Church," page 58.

Teacher's References:

Little Ones, "God Knows and Sees All," page 57.

Practical Aids, "Good Intention," page 266; "Spending the Day Well," page 80; "A Child's Rule of Life," page 79; "A Child's Christian Day," page 79; "The Little Flower Goes to Church," page 247; "Honoring the Blessed Sacrament," page 130; "We Don't Talk in Church," page 131; "How to Make a Church, Altar, Tabernacle," pages 280–282.

Teacher Tells a Story, Vol. I, "Prayer" pages 52–58.

Teacher's Notes:

At Night
May, 3rd Week

Introduction:

Read to the children the poem, "Early Prayer," *Book of the Holy Child,* p. 72.

Let the children tell how Jesus spent His day; how they can model their actions of the day on the life of Jesus.

Presentation:

"After the day's work and play were over, Jesus, Mary, and Joseph spent the evening together. How happy they were. Often in the evenings they went to the synagogue to thank God for all He had given them during the day. Jesus walked between Mary and His dear foster father, St. Joseph."

Study the picture, if accessible, of *The Holy Family,* by Murillo; or any other showing Jesus, Mary, and Joseph walking.

"When you hear the church bells ring in the evening, Jesus is calling for you. He wants you and your mother and father to visit Him once more. He wants you to thank Him for all He has done for you during the day. Jesus loves little children and their parents when they come to Him often. Ask your father to take you to Jesus in church.

"Sometimes Jesus went visiting friends with His parents. He was always very polite and modest."

Dramatize little acts of courtesy to visitors at home.

"Jesus played with His little friends in the evenings, too. Do you think He ever ran about the streets far from home? No,

Jesus loved His parents too much. He would not let them worry about Him (develop the thought somewhat):

"What Jesus loved most of all was to stay at home with His Mother Mary and good St. Joseph. St. Joseph sat and read from holy books to Mary and Jesus. Mary sat on the step sewing, while dear little Jesus was at her feet. Often He would lay His head in her lap. Then Mary smoothed His curls. Jesus would say to His dear Mother, 'My dear Mother, I love you so much.' And sweet Mother Mary would say, 'Jesus, my God and my Darling Boy.' The holy angels from heaven watched over them. They adored their little God, Jesus. Jesus often told Mary and Joseph about His Father in heaven, about the Holy Ghost, and about His beautiful heaven. When it became dark, Jesus knew that it was time to go to bed.

"He had one more thing to do before the day was over: to say His night prayer. The Holy Family sang a beautiful hymn to God, knelt down and said their night prayer out loud. Jesus said to St. Joseph, 'Good night.' Then He put His arms about His mother's neck and whispered to her: 'Good night, My sweet Mother.' Soon He was in His little bedroom and quickly went to bed. Jesus whispered one more prayer. 'My Father in heaven, bless all My little boys and girls.' Then Jesus slept and angels watched over Him all the night."

Show the picture of a child asleep with the angel guardian watching, by Tessier.

Let them repeat the prayer to the guardian angel.

Discussion on what children of their age can do in the evening. Stress especially the matter of obedience.

Children ought to be taught as early as possible in life to spend their leisure time in useful ways, reading, constructive play, music. Much of this will naturally depend upon their home environment.

Read: *The Book of the Holy Child,* "Night Prayer," page 73.

"A good little child will always tell mother or father all he has done during the day, all the good things and all the naughty things, too. Tell mother and father you are sorry that you were naughty and made them feel sad. Promise them that you will be a good child the next day. How much they will love their dear little child.

"What was the last thing Jesus did at night? What does Jesus wish you to do every night?"

Let the children recite their night prayer; teach them to think of all the naughty things they did during the day and tell God they are sorry, and promise Him to do better. Tell them to pray for all in the family; to thank God for the gifts of the day. A short prayer to Mary and to the guardian angel should not be omitted in the night prayer.

Read to the children: *The Book of the Holy Child*, "At Night," page 74.

Study the picture on page 75 and read the poem, "Good Night," by Tabb. Encourage the children to memorize it.

Let the children bring pictures of children or adults at prayer, of children at play in the home, going to bed, performing acts of courtesy, intimate home scenes. Have them make posters with these. While doing so, always keep Jesus their Model in some way before their minds.

Pupil's Readings:

American Cardinal Reader, I, "Night Prayer," page 176.

Catholic Child, I, "Good Night," page 138.

Let the children find readings in various books of the first grade and read them to the class or privately.

Teacher's References:

Practical Aids, "A Child's Christian Day," page 79; "Help of the Guardian Angel," page 79; "How to Spend the Day Well," page 80; and "How to End the Day," page 82.

Teacher's Notes:

Christ in the Temple
May, 3rd and 4th Weeks

Introduction:

"Jesus, the dear Son of Mary, grew up to be a healthy, happy Boy. Mary and Joseph loved Him daily more and more. Mary loved His beautiful eyes, His sunny hair, His sweet, gentle face. She watched Him at His work. How often Mary whispered to Him: 'My dear Jesus, I love You.' "

Study the picture, *The Boy Christ,* by Ittenbach, or Hofmann.

Note especially the beautiful features; tell the children that the expression on their face will become more like Christ's the better they become; and *vice versa.*

Presentation:

"When Jesus was twelve years old, Joseph and Mary took Him along to the city of Jerusalem to pray in the temple. The way was far and because they were poor they had to walk."

Form a procession to Jerusalem. See *Little Ones,* pages 87–90.

"But Jesus loved the temple, which was the house of God, and did not mind being tired. Every day, while they were in Jerusalem, Jesus, Mary, and Joseph went to the temple to sing and pray to God in heaven.

"After the feast days were over, Mary and Joseph started back home to Nazareth. Imagine their surprise when they found out that Jesus was not with them. Poor Mary and Joseph! They turned back and looked for their dear little Boy everywhere. They looked for Him among their friends and relatives. Their hearts were very sad. For three days they could not find Him, 'and not finding Him, they returned to Jerusalem seeking Him' (Luke ii. 45). Finally they went up to the temple. Oh, the joy in the hearts of poor Mary and Joseph! There sat Jesus among the great teachers. He was listening to them and asking them questions."

Study Hofmann's *Christ Among the Doctors.*

"They were asking Him questions, too, and were surprised at His wise answers.

"Mary and Joseph watched their little Boy and listened to His holy words. Finally they walked closer to Him and Mother Mary said: 'Son, why have You done this to us? Your father and I have looked for You sorrowing.' And Jesus said kindly: 'Why is it that you looked for Me? Did you not know that I must be about My Father's business?' Mary knew that Jesus was God. She thought of His words often and kept them in her heart.

"Jesus went back with His parents to Nazareth, and He was subject to them (Luke ii. 51). He became a carpenter like St. Joseph. He helped St. Joseph every day in the shop. 'He grew in age and wisdom before God and men' " (Luke ii. 52).

Let the children read "Hide and Seek," in *The Book of the Holy Child*, page 78.

Have the children repeat the various stories. Explain to them in detail the journey according to the suggested plan, if desired.

a) Leaving Home and Starting on Their Way: Use the pictures mentioned above for these reviews. Here use Plockhorst's *Journey to Jerusalem*. This part of the journey is beautifully described in *First Communion*, by Mother Loyola, pages 128–129; in *The Life of Our Lord*, by Mother Salome, pages 100–102; also in *The Little Ones*, by Mother Eaton, page 87.

Derive a practical lesson from each of the stories; here the obligation of hearing Mass on Sundays and holydays; thanksgiving and joy for the privilege of belonging to the true Church of Christ.

b) The Entrance into the Temple: Jesus' obligation for the first time to go to the temple of Jerusalem to adore God. Repeat the obligation of hearing Mass on Sundays and holydays. Speak to the children of taking holy water and making the genuflection properly, of saying a prayer of adoration when genuflecting. See *Little Ones*, page 89; *Jesus of Nazareth*, pages 92–93; and *First Communion*, page 139.

c) Jesus in the Temple: His prayer and offering; His attention to the instruction of the doctors; His questions to them; His beautiful deportment in the house of His Father, the temple.

Speak to the children of the real presence of Jesus in the tabernacle; how He sees all they do and pray; how He looks for them when they are able to be in church (Luke ii. 41–52); *First Communion*, pages 138–144; *Jesus of Nazareth*, page 93.

d) The Loss in the Temple: Tell the children how Joseph and Mary went in separate groups and that each thought Jesus was in the other group. How Jesus stayed in the temple because it was His Father's will. Speak of the sorrow that Jesus felt for causing His parents grief, but that He must obey His Father.

Tell the children how we lose Jesus by doing wrong; how by an act of sorrow we will find Him again; also the sorrow we should show our parents if we have done wrong.

The teacher will recite here: "A Mother's Quest," by Hunt; dramatize the various parts. True the children can hardly understand it all, but a beautiful reading will make a lasting impression. *The Little Ones*, page 87; *Jesus of Nazareth*, page 94; *First Communion*, page 144; and *Life of Jesus*, page 103.

e) The Finding of the Child Jesus: Repeat and have the children repeat the story of the anguish of the Blessed Mother and St. Joseph; how again and again they asked if anyone had seen their Jesus; finally, their return to the temple and the consequent finding of Jesus. Use Hofmann's *Christ in the Temple*, or any other art picture. Explain the words of Jesus and Mary.

Speak of the joy of our finding Jesus after sin through confession and act of contrition and the joy of Jesus and Mary at finding us again. *Jesus of Nazareth*, pages 94 and 95; *First Communion*, page 145; *Life of Our Lord*, pages 105–107.

f) The Return Home: Tell of the obedience of Jesus in returning home, the prayers and conversation on the way home; also how the Doctors often looked for Jesus in the temple because they wanted to hear more from Him. Explain the two quotations underlined in the lesson; especially "And He was subject to them." Memorize these. *Jesus of Nazareth*, pages 95–97; *First Communion*, page 145; *Life of Our Lord*, pages 107–109.

Have the children collect pictures of the childhood of Jesus and mount in a booklet.

Let the children tell the stories again and again. Let them

dramatize the various scenes. With what joy and reverence they will do it! Have them use the direct quotations, if possible.

Finally read the lesson, "On the Way to Jerusalem," in *The Book of the Holy Child*, page 76, and study the picture of the lesson.

Teacher's References:

The Little Ones, "The Loss in the Temple," pages 87–90.

Jesus of Nazareth, Chapter XII, "In the Temple Again."

First Communion, Chapter XI, "In the Temple."

Life of Our Lord, Chapter III, "The Three Days' Loss."

Practical Aids, "Jesus Goes to the Temple," page 110; "The Journey from Nazareth to Jerusalem," page 111; "The Child Jesus is Lost," page 111; "A Mother's Quest," page 112.

A Child's Garden of Religion Stories, "Lost in the Temple," pages 199–201.

The Holy Bible, St. Luke, Chapter II.

Leading the Little Ones to Christ, "Jesus at Twelve," pages 110–117.

Pictures That May Be Studied:

The Boy Jesus — Hofmann; Giovanni.

Journey to Jerusalem — Plockhorst.

Jesus Twelve Years Old, On His Way to Jerusalem — Mengelberg.

Christ in the Temple — Hofmann.

Teacher's Notes:

The Holy Family
May, 4th Week

Introduction:

Picture study of the Holy Family.

Presentation:

"After Jesus had been lost and found again, the Holy Family returned to their little home in Nazareth. How happy they were to be at home again. They had to work hard for their living. St. Joseph, the head of the Holy Family, worked in his shop from morning until night. Dear Mother Mary stayed at home and kept the house neat and clean for St. Joseph and Jesus. 'And Jesus advanced in wisdom, and age, and grace, with God and men!'" (Luke ii. 52.) The teacher will explain the text carefully.

"Soon Jesus was old and strong enough to help St. Joseph even with his hard work. They were all very happy. Mary and Joseph had Jesus, the Son of God, living with them in their little home. Just to be with Jesus is the greatest happiness on earth or in heaven. It was Jesus who made dear St. Joseph and holy Mother Mary so happy. Jesus is your little Leader. Follow Jesus and you will be happy. You, too, can do much to make your mother and father happy."

Discuss with the children how they can help to make their home happy. Always hold before them Jesus, their Model.

"Let us often pray to the Holy Family and say: 'Jesus, Mary, Joseph, I give you my heart and my soul.'"

Sing a short hymn to Jesus, one to Mary, one to Joseph.

Activities: Let the children mount a picture of the Holy Family and take it home; encourage them to explain it to their parents.

Creative Art: Paper cutting of tools, such as hammer, saw, plane, keeping in mind that Jesus worked with them to make His daily living.

These can also be modeled of clay.

Pictures That May Be Studied:

The Holy Family — Murillo.

The Holy Family — Mueller.

Pupil's Readings:

American Primer, "I Love Father," page 28; "Holy Family," page 87; "When Jesus Was a Little Boy," page 92.

American Cardinal Primer, "Holy Family," page 68.

Corona First Reader, "In the Temple," page 14; "The Holy Family," page 25,

Corona Primer, "The Home in Egypt," page 63; "At Nazareth," page 71; "Our Friends," page 74.

Ideal First Reader, "Holy Family," page 67.

Marquette First Reader, "Holy Family," page 11; "St. Joseph," page 84.

Teacher's References:

The Holy Bible, Luke ii. 52.

First Communion, Chapter X.

Jesus of Nazareth, Chapter XII, "In the Temple Again," "Death of St. Joseph," pages 100–102.

Practical Aids, "Prayer to St. Joseph," page 72 ; "Feast of St. Joseph," page 215; "Holy Family Poster," page 289; "St. Joseph Booklet," page 294.

To the Heart of the Child, "The Holy Childhood," page 55.

Teacher's Notes:

The Little Secret: Jesus, Our Leader
June, 1st and 2nd Weeks

Introduction:

Read the lesson, "The Little Secret," *The Book of the Holy Child,* page 80.

Read the poem, "Follow the Leader," in *The Child on His*

Knees, page 127, and have the children explain it. Let them memorize it.

Presentation:

"Jesus came on earth only because He loved you, His little child. He wants you to learn from Him how to live, how to be good, and how to get to heaven. Only Jesus can show you how to come to heaven. He said: 'I am the Way.' Jesus meant that you, His little child, must live the way He lived."

Discussion with the children how Jesus has shown them by His own life and actions what to do. Repeat the thoughts of obedience, prayer, kindness, mortification, sinlessness.

"Jesus said to you: 'I am the Truth.' He is God and God can never make a mistake. All that He has promised, He will do."

Speak of heaven as the reward to all good people.

"Jesus also said to you: 'I am the Life.' Jesus has given life to your body, and your soul. Jesus wants you to live for Him alone. You are still so small, but you can give your life and love to Jesus. You do this by never committing any sin and by always doing what He has done. Jesus wants your soul to be pure and holy, to be ready always to go to heaven with Him."

Talk about the beauty of a soul in grace, about the Act of Contrition cleansing the soul from venial sins.

Pictures:

Have many beautiful pictures of the Boy Jesus mounted and placed about the classroom during this lesson. Among some of the most prominent art pictures suitable for this study are:

Jesus and John — Guido Reni.
Children of the Shell — Murillo.
Divine Shepherd — Murillo.
The Christ Child — Ittenbach.
The Boy Christ — Hofmann.
The Christ Child — Feuerstein.
Light of the World — Chambers.

I Am the Way, the Truth, and the Life

Introduction:

Study the picture on page 82, *The Book of the Holy Child.*

Presentation:

"School is almost over for this year. If you have been good you are the little lamb at Jesus' side. How much He loves you. His hand is touching you with love. How close He lets you come to Him. See how proud Jesus is of His good little lamb. He has been leading you all year and He wants to lead you during the vacation. He wants you to stay very near to Himself during the summer."

Speak to the children about the following topics: vacation; obligation of hearing Mass on Sundays; daily prayer; the Act of Contrition at night; good companionship; any other topic that the teacher thinks necessary.

"Jesus wants to lead you all through your life, until He will at last take you, His good little child, into heaven to be happy with Him, your little Leader, forever."

Arrange a statue or picture of the Boy Jesus in a pretty setting. Let the children kneel before it while they read, "A Little Boy's Gift," *The Book of the Holy Child,* page 83.

Program: Jesus Our Leader

Let the last recitation periods be a program in honor of Jesus our little Leader. Have this program as a review of the year's work, each child participating in some way. Let them feel that it is all in honor of Jesus their Leader, and that they want to please Him only.

Have a statue of the Infant Jesus decorated and placed in the front of the room during the last week of school, and during this program. The following is merely suggestive:

Song:

"Dear Little One" — class.

Life of Jesus:

"The Annunciation," dramatization.

"The Visitation" — story told by child ⎫ showing
"The Nativity" — story told by child ⎭ the picture

Poems:

"A Little Child at the Crib" — child before the statue.

"Jesus Answers from the Crib" — child before the statue.

Song:

"Baby Jesus Smiling" — solo by a good singer in the class.

Song:

"Come, Gather Here, Children" — class.

Life of Jesus (continued):

"The Angels and Shepherds" — dramatization.

"The Three Kings" — dramatization.

"Christ's Presentation" — story told by child with picture.

Poem:

"Gifts," Rosetti — child.

Life of Jesus (continued):

"Flight into Egypt" — story told by child with picture.

"Return to Nazareth" — story told by child with picture.

"Christ in the Temple" — story told by child with picture.

End with a Song.

UNIT VIII

THE OUR FATHER

Introductory Remarks:

The Our Father should be taught to the children very slowly. One petition of the Our Father with explanations is sufficient for one day. To demand of children the memorization by mere rote is both unsound pedagogically and harmful to true devotion.

In this course in religion a good study of the Our Father can be made independently of any unit. It should be well reviewed during the study of Part VI, lesson on Jesus at Prayer.

Illustrated books on the Our Father are of great value in the teaching of the prayer; especially noteworthy is *The Lord's Prayer,* by Frederick M. Lynk, S.V.D. Profusely illustrated, the Mission Press, Techny, Ill.

Posters illustrating each petition of the Our Father can be made and kept before the pupils during the study of the respective petition.

At times take one or the other petition and talk informally about it with the children.

Introduction:

"Jesus often prayed. One day He was praying again. His face was turned toward His Father in heaven. His friends watched Jesus pray. When He had finished His prayer, these good friends of Jesus said: 'Lord, teach us how to pray.' Jesus was happy because He wanted His friends to pray to God the Father in heaven, too. Jesus said to them: 'When you pray, say: Our Father, who art in heaven,' etc. Dear children, that is the most beautiful prayer we can say. Jesus, God Himself, told us that prayer. Jesus wants us to say it all through our life. We will start to learn Jesus' own prayer today." (During the telling of any story, the

117

teacher should repeat and have the children repeat the respective petitions verbatim again and again.)

Presentation:

"Our Father: God is the Father of all of us. He created us. We are His very own children. God is the Father of everyone on earth — Chinese, Japanese, Indians, Negroes. We are all sisters and brothers in God's big family.

"Who art in heaven: Heaven is so beautiful that no one can describe it. It is God's special home. He wants us all to come to heaven with Him. Only good people will go to heaven" (Chisholm, *The Catechism in Examples:* "Our Father who art in Heaven," pages 74–108).

"Hallowed be Thy Name: The Name of God is the holiest word that can be said. Whenever we say the Name of God, of Jesus, all the angels in heaven adore God. We must praise the Name of God and only say it in prayer and in holy talks. That is what the word 'hallowed' means — praised, honored, loved, be the Name of God" (*op. cit.:* "Hallowed be Thy Name," pages 109–145).

"Thy Kingdom come: God is the great powerful King who made heaven and earth, who made all men and angels. We must adore our King so that one day He will take us into heaven. Every man's heart should be pure and holy because it belongs to God. That is God's kingdom on earth. Now not all men let God live in their hearts; some let the devil live in them. They commit sin and so drive their King, God, out of their hearts. When they die, God cannot take those bad people into His kingdom, heaven. When we say 'Thy Kingdom Come,' we pray that God will pardon these bad people; that He will live again in their hearts and take them with Him to heaven" (*op. cit.:* "Thy Kingdom Come," pages 146–180).

"Thy will be done on earth as it is in heaven: To do the will of God is always to do what is right and to accept anything He sends us — joy, sorrow, pain or pleasure, sickness, health, death. We ask God to help us and everyone else on earth to do His holy

will. Only if we do what God wants us to do, will we reach heaven. In heaven, everybody is happy to obey God all the time" (*op. cit.:* "Thy Will be Done," page 81).

"*Give us this day our daily bread:* When we say these words, we ask our good Father in heaven to give us all that we need to live and to remain good. We ask for all our food, not for bread only. Then, too, we ask God for Holy Communion, the food of our soul" (*op. cit.:* "Give us this Day . . .," pages 217–254).

"*Forgive us our trespasses:* Trespasses is just a big word for sins. We mean forgive us our sins. We are asking God's pardon, making an act of sorrow, for the many, many sins we have committed.

"*As we forgive those who trespass against us:* At times our playmates offend us. We must forgive them and not be angry at them. We must forget all about it even if they have not been sorry. God will forgive us our sins only if we forgive the wrong others have done us" (*op. cit.:* "Forgive . . .," pages 255–289).

"*Lead us not into temptation:* We should always do what is right. Sometimes we would like to do what is naughty. A big, red apple is on another boy's desk. The devil says to you, 'Take it, nobody will see you.' A little voice in you says, 'No, don't take it. It is not yours. You will offend God.' The devil is *tempting* you to do wrong. When we say, 'Lead us not into temptation.' we are praying to God always to help us to do the right thing, no matter how hard the *temptation* is" (*op. cit.:* pages 290–325).

"*But deliver us from evil:* These words mean that we ask God to free us from anything that could harm us in our soul or in our body. The greatest evil and the only one that can harm our soul is sin.

"Evils that harm the body are sickness, fire, robbers. We ask our good Father in heaven to free us from all evils of body and soul, so we can serve Him better" (*op. cit.:* pages 326–360).

Teacher's References:

The Little Ones, "The Our Father," pages 62–67.

Teacher Tells A Story, "The Lord's Prayer," pages 46–75.

The Catechism in Examples, Rev. D. Chisholm, "The Our Father," pages 74–360.

Teacher's Handbook to the Catechism, "The Lord's Prayer," Rev. A. Urban, pages 186–198, 252–256.

The Roman Catechism.

UNIT IX
LITURGICAL UNIT

As the feasts of the year occur, the teacher will tell the children the corresponding story of our Lord, of the Blessed Virgin Mary, of the saints, very simply. Only those events in the life of the saint should be taken which have an especial appeal to children. Pictures would add much to the understanding and interest of the child. Even though the children cannot and need not, remember all the facts, still through telling the saint stories attractively, the germ for true hero worship is taking root in their souls. The saints have been the heroes and heroines of their age. What a grand heritage falls to the Catholic child through the noble lives of God's favored ones. The life of every truly great person is a precious inspiration to every good man.

"We cannot look, however imperfectly, upon a great man without gaining something by Him. He is the living light-fountain, which it is good and pleasant to be near. The light which enlightens, which has enlightened the darkness of the world; and this not as a kindled lamp only, but rather as a natural luminary shining by the gift of Heaven; a flowing light-fountain of native original insight, of manhood and heroic nobleness — in whose radiance all souls feel that it is well with them."[1]

In real truth this can be said of God's saints. There is an inspiration in the life of every saint of God for every sincere child of the Church. Let us, the teachers of youth, place before youth from their earliest childhood ideals of their own brothers and sisters in Christ, the saints of God.

In the second semester a simple booklet on the saints could be made, composed of pictures, drawings, short sentences about the saints, the month, and its dedication.

---

[1]Carlyle, Thomas, *Heroes and Hero Worship*, page 2.

Colors of Vestments

In this grade the children's attention should be especially called to the vestments of the priest. The liturgical significance of each color is told and illustrated especially with reference to the simple stories told as required in this grade. The general divisions of the liturgical year will also be indicated and learned.

GRADE I

September — Month of the Holy Cross

September 8 — Birthday of the Blessed Virgin Mary.
September 12 — Holy Name of Mary.
September 29 — St. Michael, the archangel.

October — Month of Angels

October 2 — Guardian Angel.
October 3 — St. Thérèse, The Little Flower.
October 15 — St. Theresa.

November — Month of Poor Souls

November 1 — All Saints.
November 2 — All Souls.
November 19 — St. Elizabeth of Hungary.
November 21 — Presentation of the Blessed Virgin.

December — Month of the Holy Infant

December 8 — Immaculate Conception.
December 25 — Christmas.

January — Month of the Holy Child

January 1 — Circumcision of Jesus.
January 6 — Epiphany of our Lord.

February — Month of the Holy Family

February 2 — Candlemas Day.
February 3 — St. Blaise.
February 14 — St. Valentine.

March — Month of St. Joseph

March 17 — St. Patrick.
March 19 — St. Joseph.
March 24 — St. Gabriel.
March 25 — Annunciation of the Blessed Virgin Mary.

April — Month of the Boyhood

April 7 — Blessed Herman Joseph.
April   — Resurrection of our Lord.

May — Month of the Blessed Virgin Mary

May 12 — St. Imelda.
          Mother's Day.
          Ascension of our Lord.
          Mention here the Assumption of the Blessed Virgin
            Mary.

June — Month of the Sacred Heart

June 13 — St. Anthony of Padua.
June 21 — St. Aloysius.
June 24 — St. John the Baptist.
          Corpus Christi.

UNIT X

SPECIAL UNIT FOR FIRST HOLY COMMUNION

To the Teacher of the First Communion Class

These units on confession, Holy Mass, and Holy Communion have been written to be used in both private and solemn Communion classes.

For the private Communion class, which usually is composed of the youngest children, the teacher will not enter into details, especially in the unit of the Holy Mass. Only those points are to be taken which are essential. The mind of the little child is not to be burdened with facts which will be learned gradually as he grows older. The important idea for these little children is the love of Christ for them; hence all details, unnecessary at this age, will be omitted.

For the solemn Communion class, which is composed at large of children of the intermediate grades, as many of the details can be taken as the teacher finds her class capable of understanding. Again not the amount of information is of paramount importance, but the love of Christ in the Eucharist for the soul of man.

The reading lists for these units have been selected for Grade III; the readers of all other grades also contain stories of Holy Communion, of Holy Mass, of Confession. The readers should all be suitable to the specific class under instruction. The children should have free access to them, and also to many other beautiful books on Holy Mass, Holy Communion, and Confession.

This unit is intended for Grades I or II, wherever the pastor requires preparation for Holy Communion in these grades. If this preparation is left until the third grade, the material contained in the text for that grade, the *"Life of the Soul"* is ample.

CONFESSION

IN PREPARATION FOR FIRST HOLY COMMUNION

Teacher's Readings:

Readings for the teacher before starting the work with the children:

First Confession, Mother Loyola.

The Children's Charter, pages 1–47, Mother Loyola.

The Little Ones, Mother M. Eaton, "Confession," pages 122–131.

Any other approved book on children's confession.

Pictures:

The Sheep Rescued — Plockhorst.

The Prodigal Son — Molitor.

The Divine Shepherd — Murillo.

Christ and the Sinner — Hofmann.

The above pictures or others of a similar theme should be placed before the children for the purpose of instilling confidence in their hearts and to show the love of Jesus for all sinners but especially for themselves.

Introduction I:

Tell the story how Christ appeared to His Apostles, and said: "Peace be to you! Receive ye the Holy Ghost. Whose sins you shall forgive, they are forgiven them: and whose sins you shall retain, they are retained" (John xx. 21–23).

A general talk to the children on the goodness and love of Jesus for each child; how each one can show his love for Jesus by keeping his heart free from sins; how Jesus wants to forgive him, if he has already committed sins; how sad Jesus feels when His child has done wrong; how Jesus still loves him and has given him a way to make his soul pure again; how in confession Jesus forgives all the sins of His child, if he is sorry for them and has told them to the priest; how the priest says, "I absolve you from all your sins," and how then Jesus bends down to give His dear little child the kiss of forgiveness; how his soul will be pure and holy again after confession; how all children should love to go to Jesus in confession and have their sins forgiven.

Instruction I:

Tell the stories of the Good Shepherd and the Prodigal Son. While so doing, show the children the pictures and let them talk freely about them. Apply the story continually to the children themselves.

Oral talks by the children on the two stories.

Let the children dramatize the Prodigal Son.

Have the children read and retell to the class the following:

"The Prodigal Son," *Columbus Reader*, III, page 69;

"Penance," *Our Sacraments* — Kelly, pages 245–260;

"The Prodigal Son," *Ideal Catholic Reader*, III, page 229;

"The Little Gray Lamb," *American Third Reader*, page 161;

"The Good Shepherd," *Rosary Third Reader*, page 234.

Prayer to the Holy Ghost
Examination of Conscience

Teacher's Readings:

First Confession, Mother Loyola, Chapter I, "What We Must Do when Our Souls Are Sick"; Chapter II, "Getting Ready For Confession," pages 23–37.

Introduction:

Repeat the part of the story of the Prodigal Son as he thought of all the bad things he had done; how he made up his mind to go home to his dear father and tell him everything. The child, too, must think of the sins he has committed, so that he will know what to tell Jesus at confession.

Instruction:

Thoughts to be developed by the teacher and discussed with the children:

1. Because a child cannot think of all his sins without the help of God, the first thing to do is to ask God for help. The Holy Ghost, the Third Person of the Blessed Trinity, will enter the soul with His light if the child prays devoutly to Him. He will show the child the sins he has committed. Prayer to the Holy Ghost, *Baltimore Catechism*, No. 2, page 21.

2. Prayer to Jesus in the Blessed Sacrament; to Mary; to the Guardian Angel for help to make a good confession.

3. Examination of Conscience:

> Did I commit a big sin?
> Did I miss my morning and evening prayers? How often?
> Did I take the name of God in vain? How often?
> Did I curse or swear? How often?
> Did I miss Mass on Sunday? How often?
> Did I disobey my father or mother? How often?
> Did I fight with others? How often?
> Did I get angry? How often?
> Did I think, talk, or do bad or immodest things? How often?
> Did I cause others to do bad or immodest things? How many times?
> Did I steal anything? How much?
> Did I spoil anything belonging to anyone else? How much?
> Did I tell lies? How often?
> Did I talk badly about others? How often?
> Did I eat meat on Friday? How often?
> Is there anything else I ought to tell?

When we come to the examination of conscience we are on somewhat slippery ground, and must be careful and discreet. Though the confession of mortal sins alone is of obligation, we shall do well not to lay too much stress on this, but encourage the children to tell whatever sins they remember. Pass quickly over the Sixth Commandment, taking care not to bring before their minds anything suggestive of evil. Be satisfied with showing what has to be done in case anything should cause trouble in any direction. To say sufficient for the needs of all, yet not too much for one particular child, is perhaps difficult. But the safest plan is to get the children to have confidence in the priest, who, because he is in the place of our Lord, will always be kind and comforting. Say what we should tell him without fear, if anything makes us feel unhappy. He knows all about people's troubles, and he will help make us happy again directly.

We must ask the Holy Spirit to put the right words on our lips when we come to this subject, or it may happen that in seeking to avoid one rock we fall upon another. A child warned of the sacrilege of hiding a mortal sin through shame, might through a false conscience be led to commit a sacrilege by hiding what was no sin at all. *First Confession* — Mother Mary Loyola, page 15.

4. God loves His child in spite of all the sins. He knows and has seen all that has happened. He wants him to tell in the confessional all the big sins, and then all the smaller ones that he remembers.

Read, explain, and discuss with the children the poem, "Come to Jesus," Faber.

Teach the children to make an examination of conscience every night.

Let the children read and retell to the class the following:

Ideal Catholic Reader, III, "Why Rose Couldn't Sleep," page 151.

Columbus, III, "Whatever Are Your Faults," page 36.

Sorrow and the Purpose of Amendment

Teacher's special reference: *First Confession* — Mother Loyola, Chapter II, pages 37–56, "Sorrow."

Pictures:

Christ's Agony in the Garden — Hofmann.

The Crucifixion — Hofmann, Guido Reni, Van Dyke.

St. Peter Repentant — Dolci.

Mary Magdalen, the Penitent — Hofmann.

The Prodigal Son — Molitor.

Introduction:

Repeat the story of the Prodigal Son's return and his act of sorrow. Use the direct words of his act of contrition: "Father, I have sinned against Heaven and before thee. I am not worthy to be called thy son." Show the picture to the children and dwell especially on his deep sorrow; apply the lesson to the children.

Tell briefly the stories of St. Peter and Mary Magdalen. Stress their intense sorrow because they had offended Jesus. Speak of their lifelong repentance.

Instruction:

Thoughts to be developed by the teacher and discussed with the children:

1. The most important thing in confession is sorrow. No sin, not even the smallest, can be forgiven without sorrow.

2. Show the picture of the Crucifixion and tell the children that sin, especially mortal sin, made Jesus suffer.

3. They have sorrow for their sins if they are sorry that they have offended God; that they have caused the sufferings and death of Jesus; that they have lost heaven by their big sins and deserved hell.

4. They must promise God they will try never again to commit these sins.

5. Pray to Jesus for help to make a good act of sorrow.

6. Daily practice of making an act of sorrow at night; also immediately after committing any sin; saying the ejaculation: My Jesus, Mercy, often.

7. Read to the children and discuss with them the poems: "God is Full of Pity," Garesché; "Staying Away," Thayer.

8. Let the children read and tell to the class: *A Child's Garden of Religion Stories,* "Penance," page 155; "Against the Devil and Sin," page 232.

9. Teach the children the Act of Contrition, *Baltimore Catechism,* No. 2, page 22.

Confession and the Atonement

Teacher's Special References:

First Confession, Chapter III, "In the Confessional," page 57.

First Confession, Chapter IV, "Thanksgiving After Confession," page 60.

Pictures:

Christ, the Consoler — Plockhorst.

Introduction:

Repeat the story of the Prodigal Son. Dwell on the confession of the Prodigal; his sincerity; his promise never again to commit those sins. Show the picture of the Prodigal Son once more and now stress the kindness of the good old father.

Apply the lesson to the children by showing them the picture, *Christ, the Consoler,* and explaining that Jesus and the child alone are in the confessional since the priest just takes the place of Jesus; speak of the love of Jesus for His child; of the kiss of forgiveness Jesus gives His child.

Instruction:

Thoughts to be developed by the teacher and discussed with the children:

1. The priest takes the place of God. The priest forgives sins because our Lord gave him the power to do so.

2. God knows all the sins the child has committed; He wants the child to tell them to the priest just as he has committed them.

Remember the priest will never be angry with you. He will never tell. He will help you. But never leave a big sin out or tell a lie about it because you are afraid. If you have tried your best and have forgotten a sin, it was forgiven with the rest. Only, if you remember it afterwards you must confess it the next time you go to confession. But if you hid a big sin because you were afraid, God would be very angry with you. You would not get any of your sins forgiven. You would be very miserable. The next time you went to confession, you would have to tell that sin, and also that you had hidden it in the former confession. Never leave out any sin that makes you especially unhappy. Say to the priest: "Father, help me tell my sins because I am afraid." *First Confession,* Mother Loyola, pages 37 and 38.

3. Confession of the big sins first and then the smaller ones.

4. Listen quietly to what the priest says. When the priest does not speak to you, say the Act of Sorrow.

5. Every question that the priest asks must be answered honestly.

6. Forgiveness makes the soul pure again.

7. When the priest says: "Go in peace"; or "God bless you," leave the confessional modestly and go into a pew near the Blessed Sacrament.

8. Say the prayers the priest told you to say. Jesus wants you to say them, otherwise He will not forgive your sins. Promise Jesus again that you will never commit a big sin. Ask the Blessed Virgin Mary and your guardian angel to help you keep your soul pure. Tell Jesus that you will avoid all sins, but especially the one that you commit oftenest.

9. Thank God once more by saying a few short prayers to Him.

10. Frequent Confession, for children, once in two weeks.

Development:

1. Constant drill of the prayers and how to tell the sins.

2. If this is the First Confession, let the children see the confessional and kneel down in it to take away any fear and strangeness. Teach them to wait their turn to go to confession.

3. Children read and tell to the class the following: *Columbus,* III, "The Good Samaritan," page 155. *Ideal Catholic Reader,* III, "Jesus Heals the Lepers," page 104.

Teacher's General References:

First Confession, Mother Loyola.

The Faith for Children, Mary Eaton, "Penance," page 129; "Sorrow," page 132; "Effects of," page 137; "Satisfaction," page 138; "Thanksgiving," page 140.

The Little Ones, Mary Eaton, "Confession," pages 123–131.

Teacher Tells A Story, Vol. I, Hannan, "Holy Ghost," page 107; "Confiteor," pages 94–101; Vol. II, pages 181–184.

To the Heart of the Child, Brownson, "Confession," page 86.

The Form of Confession

The penitent says:

Bless me, Father. In the name of the Father, and of the Son, and of the Holy Ghost, Amen.

I confess to Almighty God and to you, Father, that I have sinned.

This is my first confession, or I went to confession —— weeks, months, ago.

These are my sins: ————

For these and all my sins which I cannot now remember, I ask pardon of God, and the penance and absolution from you, Father.

Listen to the priest.

When the priest prays, say the Act of Contrition.

After the priest says, "God bless you" or "Go in peace," leave the confessional and modestly go to your place in church. Thank Jesus for forgiving your sins.

Say your penance.

Short admonitions at varying intervals for confession:

"Dear children, a beautiful day is coming tomorrow. Jesus wants you to come to Him to confession. What a happy day for you! Jesus loves you so much. He wants to take every little and big spot off your soul. He wants to make your soul the most beautiful thing on earth. You have committed sins and now Jesus sees those sins on your soul. Oh, He wants to have your soul beautiful and clean, and to give it more and more grace. How good Jesus is to you. Try your best tomorrow to show Jesus how thankful you are to Him."

Now review as far as necessary for the class.

A BRIEF STUDY OF THE MASS IN PREPARATION FOR FIRST HOLY COMMUNION

The Bread of Life

Teacher's Readings:

Teacher's special reading in preparation for this unit on the Mass: *Eucharistia,* Rev. J. Kramp, S.J.

Pictures:

Christ Feeding the Multitude — Murillo.

The Last Supper — da Vinci.

The First Mass — Joseph Aubert.

Preparing For Holy Mass — Louis Emile Adan.

Introduction:

Show the picture, *Christ Feeding the Multitude.* Tell the story to the children, making it very vivid, showing the almighty power of Jesus, who is God.

Presentation:

"The next day the people came to Jesus in large numbers. They thought Jesus would feed them again. When Jesus saw why they were coming, He was sad. He told them kindly not to work for this life only, but for eternal life. Then He made the most wonderful promise. Jesus said to them: 'I am the bread of life. If any man eat of this bread, he shall live forever' (John vi. 48, 52). He promised that He would give them Himself in the Blessed Sacrament. Dear children, soon Jesus is coming to you in Holy Communion. Keep your soul pure and holy for He is waiting to come into it. Often whisper to your Jesus: 'Oh, Jesus, I want You so much. Please help me to prepare well for You.' "

Let the children repeat the story of the feeding of the five

133

thousand, using pictures to help them. Also a dramatization of the various scenes would be suitable.

Let the children repeat the story of the promise and the feeding of the five thousand.

"Jesus was soon going back to His Father in heaven. He had to die upon the cross to open the gate of heaven for all of us. Jesus had promised to give Himself to His children on earth. Now the night before He died, He kept the promise that He had made."

Show the picture of the Last Supper again and again. The children love to repeat these stories.

The Mass in General

Pictures:

The Crucifixion — Hofmann.

Preparing for Holy Mass — Louis Emile Adan.

Introduction:

Teach the children a simple hymn to the Blessed Sacrament. (For beautiful, simple, devotional songs for little children see *The Child's Book of Hymns,* Sisters of Charity, Dubuque, Iowa, approved by Dr. Otto Singenberger. See Bibliography.)

Instruction on the Mass:

Thoughts to be developed by the teacher and discussed with the children:

1. The first Mass was said by Jesus Christ, the Son of God, at the last supper.

Show the picture of the first Mass and study it carefully.

2. The Sacrifice of Calvary and the Sacrifice of Mass are the very same; that of Calvary is the bloody sacrifice of the Body and Blood of Jesus; that of the Mass is the unbloody sacrifice of the Body and Blood of Jesus.

Picture study of the Crucifixion. Keep before the children the truth that the Sacrifice of the Cross and the Mass are the same.

3. The Mass is the greatest sacrifice that can be offered to God. The Mass is our Sacrifice.

4. Mass is said every moment of the day and night somewhere on this earth, a continual sacrifice.

Gather pictures from missionary magazines of priests in the missions, of the huts used for churches, of the different races present at the one same Sacrifice, the Mass. Have the children mount these pictures.

5. The Value of the Mass.

6. Attendance at Mass on Sundays and holydays of obligation a strict command of the Church under the pain of mortal sin.

7. Attendance at daily Mass encouraged as a preparation for First Communion; also to show love and gratitude to God.

8. Children should pray the Mass.

If the children have the book, *A Child's True Story of Jesus,* by Sister M. Ambrose, let them paste their Mass pictures into it just as the lessons develop.

9. Perfect deportment at Mass for love of Jesus.

The Three Principal Parts of the Mass

Pictures:

Mass pictures from *A Child's True Story of Jesus,* Sister Mary Ambrose, O.P. (See Bibliography.)

Cain and Abel — Doré.

Sacrifice of Abraham — Rembrandt.

The Last Supper — da Vinci.

Introduction:

Always show the Mass pictures in connection with the study of any part of the Mass. Slides available from Co-op Parish Activities Service, Effingham, Ill.

Instruction:

Thoughts to be developed by the teacher and discussed with the children:

1. Offertory: Tell the children of the sacrifices of Cain and Abel; of Abraham; of Christ's own offering on Calvary. After saying the short prayers in their Mass book, encourage them to recite to Jesus quietly the little poems they have learned, such as "Gifts," Rosetti; *A Little Boy's Gift,* Hope Cecil. Through these they can offer their heart to God with the offering of the

priest. They should make their penny offering on Sunday for love of Jesus. Suggest to have their prayer book and offering ready on Saturday night so as not to forget.

2. Consecration: After the little bell has rung three times, it is nearly time for Jesus to come down on the altar from heaven. How happy the little child who will be in church when Jesus comes.

When the priest says "This is My Body; this is My Blood," the bread and wine are changed into the Body and Blood of Christ. This is a great miracle.

The priest holds Jesus in the little white Host high so all the people in Church can see Him and adore Him. Look at the Host. It is now Jesus. He blesses you. Say to Him: "My Lord and my God." Jesus smiles at all good children from the Sacred Host.

Tell the story once more of the Last Supper; also of the death of Christ on Calvary. Show pictures of both.

3. Communion: Tell the children the story of the Apostles' First Communion at the Last Supper. Show a picture of the scene. Speak of the joy, the devotion, the gratitude of the Apostles. Their faces show their happiness and purity.

After the little bell has rung three times again, our Lord enters the heart of the priest in Holy Communion. He wishes to come to all pure hearts. The priest then brings Jesus to all the people who go to Holy Communion. Tell Jesus you, too, want to receive Him. Ask Him to help you prepare well for your First Holy Communion.

Encourage frequent Communion.

The Minor Parts of the Mass
For Older Children

Pictures:

Mass pictures from *A Child's True Story of Jesus*, books I, II, or III, Sister Mary Ambrose, O.P.

My Mass Book, Sister Servants of the Immaculate Heart of Mary.

Introduction:

Hymn to the Blessed Sacrament.

Instruction:

Thoughts to be developed:

Confiteor: The soul in the presence of God and all the heavenly court acknowledges its unworthiness and begs forgiveness from God and the intercession of the saints.

Kyrie: A prayer of intense pleading that God may have mercy on His people.

Gloria: The first of this hymn of joy was sung by the angels at the birth of Christ. This is a hymn full of praise to God.

Gospel: The word of God, the life of Jesus and His divine teaching. Speak of the reverence of the Church in requiring the people to stand when the Gospel is read. Call attention to the triple cross, the one on the forehead, to know Christ; the one on the lips, to speak of Christ; the one on the heart, to have the life of Christ in us.

Credo: The chief truths of the Catholic Faith. We should say the Creed to make our act of faith before the heavenly court.

Sanctus and Benedictus: This is another prayer of praise to God. It is full of joy and expectation for the King who will soon come down on His throne, the altar.

Pater Noster: The priest looks at the Sacred Host and recites the greatest, most beautiful prayer in the world, the Our Father, the Lord's own prayer.

Agnus Dei: Another beautiful prayer for mercy, for forgiveness of sin, before we receive Holy Communion.

O Lord, I am not worthy: Communion time is here. The priest takes Jesus into his hand and three times acknowledges before heaven and earth his unworthiness to receive Holy Communion. In the same prayer he places entire trust in Christ and so receives Him into his heart.

Blessing: Mass is almost over. Once more God wishes to bless us for the day. God will reward us for attending Mass by His blessing for the work of the day.

Last Gospel: We give final honor to the word of Christ, a part of His Gospel is read again and we stand in triumph at the completion of the greatest miracle God has ever performed, the sacrifice of the Mass.

If the children have the book, *A Child's True Story of Jesus,* let them paste their Mass pictures into it just as the lessons develop.

Articles Necessary for Mass
The Altar Table

In the following Instructions only the most important articles should be mentioned to little children. All have been placed into the outline for those classes of children preparing for their Solemn Holy Communion, occurring usually in the intermediate grades. To the little children in the primary grades, only the few most prominent articles, sacred vessels, and vestments should be explained.

Pictures:

All the pictures of the Mass as used in the previous lessons.

Introduction:

A visit to the Church. After a devout act of adoration, a reverent study of the altar should take place.

Instruction:

The altar table represents the table at which our Lord instituted the Holy Eucharist and said His first Mass.

The altar stone with its crosses and relics is that part of the altar table on which the chalice must rest.

Three altar cloths of linen to show deep respect to the Blessed Sacrament.

The crucifix must be over the altar, because the Sacrifice of the Mass is the same as the Sacrifice on Calvary.

The candles must be lit. They represent Christ, the Light of the World.

The tabernacle, the home of Jesus in the Sacred Host, should be of gold. It must be lined and curtained with silk.

The Sacred Vessels

The chalice is used by the priest because our Lord used one at the Last Supper. It is usually made of silver, but gold is also used. The inside of the chalice must always be gilded. The chalice is used to hold the wine which will be changed into the Blood of Christ at consecration.

The paten is the golden plate on which the bread is offered to God which at consecration is changed into the Body of Christ.

The ciborium is the golden vessel which contains the small Hosts used for the Communion of the people.

The monstrance is the beautiful golden vessel which is used at Benediction of the Blessed Sacrament.

The pyx is the golden vessel in which the priest carries the Blessed Sacrament to the sick.

Other Articles

The bread, which is cut into Hosts, must be made of wheat flour and water only. (Show the children a large host and a small one.)

The wine must be fermented grape juice because that is the kind our Lord used at the Last Supper.

The water which the priest puts into the wine, represents the water that flowed from Christ's side on the cross.

The cruets are glass flasks from which the water and wine are poured at Mass into the chalice. They are kept on the credence table.

The corporal is the square piece of linen upon which the priest lays the Host.

The vellum is the cloth covering over the chalice.

The Mass book and the altar charts contain the prayers the priest must say.

Vestments and Their Colors

Let the children see these. It would be very instructive if the priest would show the children how he puts them on and make the explanations as he does so. Otherwise the teacher will show these articles to the children and explain them.

The amice, a one-piece linen garment worn over the shoulders. It is the symbol of the armor of God.

The alb, a long white linen vestment reaching to the feet. It is a symbol of purity.

The cincture, a thick cord of linen, silk, or cotton threads. It holds up the alb. It is the symbol of chastity.

The maniple, an ornamental band of cloth worn over the left arm. It is a symbol of labor in the sacred ministry.

The stole, a long strip of ornamented silk goods, worn around the neck and fastened by the girdle in the front. It is the symbol of the duty and power of the priest.

The chasuble, the beautiful, colored outer vestment of the priest. It is a symbol of the yoke and burden of Christ.

The biretta, the covering which the priest wears on his head.

The children can make a booklet, "My Mass Book." They will cut out of religious catalogs any pictures which refer to the Mass. The booklet can be divided into four or five sections: The Altar, The Sacred Vessels, Other Articles, The Vestments, God's Kingdom on Earth. The pictures will be placed in their respective sections. A short sentence for older children, about the use of each article, can be written under each. For children in the first grade only the more prominent articles should be taken. In all this study of the Mass, let the teacher remember to use only so much of it as will be suitable to her class.

Instead of an individual booklet, large class charts could be made, all participating.

Paper cutting: The following articles can be simply cut from paper: altar, chalice, paten, linens, host with pictures of Baby Jesus pasted on it, vestments.

For the patterns of the above see *Art Education Through Religion,* Book I, page 35; Book II, pages 37 and 39; Book IV, page 39.

Clay modeling: Any of the above articles that can be modeled, altar, crucifix, candles, chalice, paten.

Class project at the close of the unit.

a) During the course of the study each child, with the help of the teacher, will have prepared a special little talk on one article used at Mass; e.g., the chalice, candles. During one of the final class periods, one child will act as chairman. He tells what the Mass is, its institution. He then calls upon others to tell any other important general things about the Mass, such as Sunday's Obligation, Mass Prayers, Deportment at Mass. The chairman calls upon each child for his contribution to the project. The child will step before the class, and with the article in hand, either in picture or in reality, or of his own handiwork, will explain its use in the Mass. For very little children it will be sufficient to state:

A crucifix must be on the altar.

Two candles must be used at Mass.

The bell is rung like this.

b) The vestments can also be introduced as the above suggests.

c) Poems, such as "Gifts," can be recited.

d) Hymns to the Blessed Sacrament should be interspersed.

Pupil's Readings:

American Cardinal Reader, III, "A Child's Wish," page 247; IV, "The Mass," page 112.

Child's Garden of Religion Stories, "Manna from Heaven."

Columbus, III, "Love of Jesus Christ," page 247.

Ideal Catholic Reader, III, "Jesus Changes Water to Wine," page 45.

Mass for Children, Father Kelley.

Rosary Reader, III, "The Chalice and the Paten," page 162; "At the Offertory," page 164; "The Color of the Vestments," page 268.

My Mass Book, Sister Servants of the Immaculate Heart of Mary.

The Wonder Gifts, Taggart, "Catholic Child," page 128.

Teacher's References:

The Holy Bible, John, Chapter 6.

Eucharistia, J. Kramp, Chapter II, "The Visible Ceremony"; Chapter III, "The Internal Structure."

The Sacrifice of the Mass, Herbst, pages 111–115.

Faith for the Children, Eton, "Sacrifices," page 154; "Vestments" page 162.

The Little Ones, M. Eaton, "The Mass," page 146.

The Mass, Father Dunney.

The Externals of the Catholic Church, Sullivan.

The Visible Church, Sullivan.

Teacher's Notes:

FIRST HOLY COMMUNION

The Last Supper

Pictures:

The Last Supper — da Vinci.

Christ Blessing Little Children — Plockhorst.

The Communicants — Jules Breton.

Christ Among the Lilies.

The Institution of the Holy Eucharist — H. Nuettsens.

Pictures from, *The Wonder Gift* — Marion Taggart.

Pope Pius and the Children.

Any other beautiful Communion pictures. *The Sacred Heart Messenger* has offered many colored pictures on this theme.

Introduction:

Review the story of the Last Supper, laying the greatest stress on the institution of the Blessed Eucharist. Show the children various mounted pictures and discuss these with them. Use the exact quotations in discussions: "This is My Body; This is My Blood."

Review also the story of Christ and the little children, stressing Christ's love for children. Show the pictures used in a previous lesson.

In both these stories stress the love of Jesus for pure hearts, especially those of children; His great longing to be with them; particularly His desire to come to them in Holy Communion.

Articles of Faith

Instruction:

Review during this week the truths that every child must know before receiving First Holy Communion:

1. God, the Creator of heaven and earth; His power; His omnipotence; His omniscience; His holiness.

2. The Blessed Trinity: one God, three Persons; God the Father created us; God the Son redeemed us; God the Holy Ghost made us holy. We cannot understand this mystery, but because God, who cannot tell a lie, has told us about it, we must believe.

Tell the story of St. Augustine and the angel.

Let the children dramatize it.

3. The Incarnation and the Redemption: Review these stories very briefly.

4. My Soul: immortal, made to the image of God. Sin destroys grace in the soul. The punishment for sin, hell; the reward for a good life, heaven; beauty of soul in grace.

5. The Holy Eucharist is the Body and Blood of Christ, the food of the immortal soul. The Sacred Host looks and tastes like bread, but it is not bread. It is the true Body and Blood of Jesus, the Son of God. It is the same Jesus who is true God from eternity; who was born in the stable and became Man; who was crucified; who redeemed us from sin.

Let the children make posters with slogans, maxims, or prayers to the Holy Eucharist; e.g., I will often receive Jesus; Holy Communion every Sunday; Offer Holy Communion for sinners; My Best to Jesus.

Also mount beautiful pictures that refer to the Mass, to the Holy Eucharist. Exhibit these in the classroom throughout the period of preparation for Holy Communion.

Immediate Preparation

Introduction:

Each day of this week tell the children a beautiful First Communion story. Among those most appealing to children are the stories of St. Imelda, St. Tarcisius, St. Gerard, St. Stanislaus Kostka, St. Aloysius, and Little Nellie of Holy God.

Let song and prayer be a part of each day's happy preparation for the great day.

Instruction:

Let the love of Jesus permeate every thought, word, deed, of both teacher and pupil. With this in mind the following suggestions are to be developed by the teacher and discussed with the pupils:

1. It is love for each child that brings Jesus down from heaven upon the altar at the consecration when the priest says: "This is My Body; this is My Blood." How Jesus is present we do not understand. This is one of God's secrets that we shall know only in heaven. We believe it because Jesus, God, told us so. Study the Act of Faith.

The children can find stories on First Communion, on the Mass, on frequent Communion and tell these to the class. The readers of the respective grades offer many of these.

2. Jesus' true home on earth is not the tabernacle, it is the heart of man. Your heart is the temple of the Holy Ghost. Every fault leaves a spot on the soul; every sin stains the soul; these spots and stains Jesus hates. You can make your soul pure again by a good confession and if the sins are small ones by a good act of contrition. Study the Act of Contrition.

3. Jesus longs to come into His true home, your heart, more than you can ever long for Him. The more you long for Jesus, the more graces He will bring when He comes to you.

Pray to the Blessed Virgin to give you as much love and longing to receive Jesus as she had for Jesus on Christmas night before He was born. Every night pray to the Blessed Virgin for more and more love to Jesus. Act of longing.

"My Prayer Book." Children write their own little prayers before and after Communion; what they want to tell Jesus or ask Him.

4. Prayers: Prepare now what you want to tell Jesus when He comes to you. Pray for yourself, for mother and father, for everybody you love. If father or mother do not go to church, pray for their conversion. Speak to Jesus and let Jesus speak to you. Listen and He will whisper something to you.

5. Be polite to Jesus. When you go to Him, don't look around, but think only of Him. When you kneel at the altar, tell Him how much you long for Him, how much you love Him. Then after you have received Him, be very polite to Him and let Him

speak to you. Leave the altar modestly and think only of Him.

Another way to be polite to Jesus is to have on very clean clothes, and to have your body perfectly clean, just like your soul. Remember your body will be just like the chalice because Jesus is in you.

6. To prepare well for Jesus every day do something just for love of Him, something that is hard for you. Jesus gives you so much on your First Communion day, you, too, ought to give Him something. The more you give Him, the happier He will be to come to you. He wants your hearts.

Suggestions of little acts of mortification, extra prayers.

Booklets: "My Gift to Jesus." Let the children make their own booklets as they please. My gift to Jesus can be a daily resolution booklet, decorated with pictures of Jesus.

7. The night before First Holy Communion speak to Jesus only.

Tell mother and father you want to speak to Jesus only; and ask them to pray for you, too. Go to bed early and repeat often, "Jesus, come to me. Jesus, I long for You. Jesus help me to receive You well."

When you awaken in the morning, think of Jesus. Talk to Jesus. Tell Him you are so happy, that you long for Him.

Ask mother and father to go to Holy Communion with you. Pray to Mother Mary in heaven and to your Guardian Angel to help you receive Jesus on this happy day.

During the day often think of dear Jesus who came to you in the morning. Thank Him again and again and promise Him that you will receive Him again very soon.

8. The teacher must speak of the two requisites of a worthy Holy Communion: freedom from mortal sin and fasting from midnight. Here the thought might also be spoken of, that they should go to Holy Communion often, but only because they love Jesus, not because other children are going. Note to the teacher: Never offer a reward to a child for going to Holy Communion. Holy Communion is its own reward. Never put up a chart numbering the Holy Communions.

Other Activities: For Solemn Communicants:

a) Form a Mission Club, choosing as patron, St. Tarcisius, St. Imelda, or any other of the saints especially devoted to the Blessed Sacrament. The children should try to earn the pennies they offer.

b) Class Discussions on: A Retreat, My Secret with Jesus (overcoming anger, practicing some virtue), General Confession, Renewal of Baptismal Vows, The Scapular, The Sodality of the Blessed Virgin Mary.

Hymns, Prayers, Practice:

The prayers, hymns, and practice periods, should form an important part of the preparation for Holy Communion. A special period should be set aside for their study and practice. While the children are learning, have them realize that this period is a period of loving preparation. They might fold their hands for a time, especially after they once know the songs and prayers, while singing or reciting them.

Prayers: Acts of Faith, Hope, Charity, Contrition, Longing.

These prayers should not be memorized, but read most carefully from the prayer book. The Sister should explain them thoroughly.

Short Acts for Holy Communion from *My Communion Book,* Austin Schmidt, S.J., Loyola Press, 25 cents, are very good.

Teach the ejaculations: Save me by Your Precious Blood; Lord, I am not worthy.

Hymns for First Holy Communion, Sister Frances, Dubuque, are simple and very beautiful hymns suitable for the youngest First Communicants.

Poems and Quotations:

This is the Bread which cometh from heaven (John vi. 50)

"In Church" — Thayer.

"Holy Communion" — Speer Strahan.

"A Child's Wish" — Father Ryan.

"First Communion" — Thayer.

"After Communion" — Thayer.

"First Communion Day" — Faber.

Pupil's Readings:

Have books on library table and let children read the stories on Holy Communion and tell them to one another.

American Cardinal, "Grandma's Gift," page 169.

Ideal, "The Sacred Heart," page 149.

Standard, "A Legend of the Fair Child," page 130.

Rosary, "Christ Our King," page 208.

Corona, "Jesus Gentlest Savior," page 177; "Jesus and the Little Children," page 91; "To the King of Heaven," page 87.

American, "Different Ways," page 125.

Child's Garden, "Bread of Everlasting Life," page 113.

American, "A Lover of Children," page 112.

Our First Communion, Father Kelly.

The Wonder Gift, Taggart.

Ideal, II, "God Heard Fred's Prayer."

American Cardinal, "Blessed Imelda," page 140; "St. Cyril," page 118.

Ideal, "First Communion," page 238.

Columbia, "Holy Communion," page 112; "The Lily," page 112.

Columbia, "Today," page 250.

Misericordia, "Blessed Imelda's First Communion," page 196; "Tarcisius," page 261.

American, IV, "My New Sister."

Child's Garden, "St. Clare," page 246; "Jesus Rewards His Beloved," page 250; "Imelda," page 271.

American Cardinal, III, "St. Tarcisius," page 239; IV (An old Woman After Holy Communion) "The Basque Song."

Misericordia, IV, "A Little Swiss Boy" (Fiddling to the Blessed Sacrament), page 113.

Teacher's References:

Encyclical of Pope Pius X, on *Holy Communion.*

Jesus of Nazareth, Mother Loyola, "The Last Supper," page 329.

Children's Charter, Mother Loyola, "Multiplication of Loaves," All of Part II, page 67.

First Communion, Mother Loyola, Part II and Part III.

The Little Ones, Mary Eaton, "The Real Presence" page 137; "Preparation for First Holy Communion," pages 142–151.

To the Heart of the Child, "Blessed Sacrament," page 121.

Little Talks to Children Preparing for Holy Communion, J. Gummersbach.

The Life of Our Lord, Mother Salome, pages 298–363.

Eucharistia, Rev. J. Kramp, S.J., Chapter IV, "Sacrificial Banquet"; Chap. V, E. Adoration; Chap. VI, E. Scheme of Life.

Stories:

Christ and the Children.

True Stories for First Holy Communion, Rev. F. Reuter, "My Happiest Day."

Herbst, "Little Nellie."

Stories for First Holy Communion, Father Herbst (taken from *Tell Us Another*): "Jesus," page 28; "Wisdom of a Little Girl," page 58; "Preserve Your White Tie," page 84; "A Beautiful Legend of H. C.," page 88; "The Wonderful Remedy," page 95; "A Modern Tarcisius," page 98; "The Very Greatest Act of Love," page 107; "I Am Not Poor," page 127; "The Reason Why," page 134.

Saints:

Tarcisius, Imelda, Aloysius, Little Flower, Gerard.

ACTS BEFORE AND AFTER COMMUNION FOR VERY YOUNG CHILDREN

Act of Faith

O my God I believe in Thee, because Thou art the Eternal Truth.

Act of Hope

O my God, I hope in Thee, because Thou art infinitely powerful, merciful, and faithful.

Act of Love

O my God, I love Thee above all things, because Thou art infinitely good and merciful.

Act of Contrition

O my God, I am sorry that I have sinned against Thee, for Thou art so good. I will never sin again. O pardon me, and help me with Thy grace.

APPENDIX

Pictures

"You must look at pictures studiously, earnestly, honestly. It will take years before you come to a full appreciation of art; but when at last you have it, you will be possessed of the purest, loftiest, and most ennobling pleasure that the civilized world can offer you." — *John Van Dyke.*

A really good picture is invaluable to every teacher. It at once draws the attention of the child, it gives a clear impression to him, stimulates his desire for imitation, and quickens his imagination. The teacher in religion should use as many pictures as possible in connection with the daily lesson. For this purpose it would be well to keep in separate files the pictures collected for each unit. The pictures should be Catholic in conception, and, if possible, attractively colored. The children also could be interested in making their collection or in adding to the school collection of pictures.

Miniature colored prints of the pictures mentioned in the various lessons may be purchased for as small a sum as one cent each. The Bibliography at the end of this Manual lists several of the firms or organizations which supply these.

A wall picture has been suggested in various lessons of this Course. The following pictures suitable for Grade I may be purchased at about the price named from church-goods and art dealers. All except one are in colors.

Title	Size	Price
Madonna of the Angels	31 by 20	$4.00
Suffer the Little Ones — Carlos Oswald	27 by 35	4.50
Christ Blessing Children — Untersberger	22 by 50	4.00
The Annunciation — Fra Angelico	18 by 25	2.50

The Nativity (white and black) — Feuerstein   22 by 28   1.20
The Holy Family Trypticon — Untersberger   20 by 30   4.00
The Guardian Angel — Carlos Oswald. . . . .   16 by 22   2.25
The Guardian Angel — Untersberger. . . . . . .   19 by 20   4.00

Other Materials

Church-goods houses can also supply paper statuettes of Christ in the crib, 100 for about $1.75, and a new paper-mâché crib set of twelve figures. Figures 2½ inches, 75 cents per set; figures 4½ inches, $2.00 per set.

The materials supplied by the Co-Op Parish Activities Service (Rev. George M. Nell, director), Effingham Ill., are deserving of special mention. Among these are:

1. The "52-Set" colored pictures.
    a) The life of Christ.
    b) The parables of our Lord.
        (The pictures of this set may be had also in miniature.)
    c) The "52-Set" teacher's manual.
2. The catechism illustrated.
3. Outline pictures, silhouettes, sand-table cut-outs in colors, gummed pictures.

Distributors of Pictures

The following series of pictures are suggested for Grade I:
Nelson: Old and New Testament, Foundation of the Church.
Tissot: New Testament (in colors).
Doré: New Testament (in colors).
Wilde: Life of Christ, Old Testament, Madonnas.
Brown: Life of Christ, Old Testament, Madonnas.
The Lienweber Collection.

The series listed above may be obtained from The Perry Pictures, Box 10, Malden, Mass., or from the New York Sunday School Commission, 416 Lafayette St., New York City. The pictures sell for from one and a half cents upward.

A Bible chart of exquisitely colored art pictures is published by Philipp Schumacher in Munich. The American agent for this chart is Rev. Conrad Hoffmann, Nazareth Hall, St. Paul, Minn.

For small individual prints for classwork and for larger prints consult the catalogs of the following distributors. Some of these firms supply descriptive guides to the pictures at about 2 cents each.

The Perry Pictures, Box 10, Malden, Mass.

Practical Drawing Company, 1315 S. Michigan Blvd., Chicago, Ill.

The University Prints, 10 Boyd St., Newton, Mass.

The Art Extension Society, Westport, Conn.

Bibliography

Art Education Through Religion, Gertrude M. McMunigle, Books I to VIII (Chicago: Mentzer, Bush and Co.).

Catechism in Examples, The (5 vols.), Rev. D. Chishom (London: Burns, Oates and Washbourne).

Child on His Knees, The, Marion Dixon Thayer (New York: The Macmillan Co., 1928), 131 pages.

Child's Book of Hymns (Dubuque, Iowa: St. Joseph's Convent, 1928), 65 pages.

Child's Garden of Religion Stories, A, Rev. P. H. Matimore (New York: Macmillan, 1929).

Child's Song Treasury, The, Mary B. Ehrmann (Cincinnati, Ohio: Willis Music Co.).

Child's True Story of Jesus, A, Sister Ambrose, O.P. (Chicago: Lawdale Publishing House, 1928).

Eucharistia, Rev. Joseph Kramp, S.J. (Tr. by Rev. Wm. Busch. St. Paul, Minn.: Lohmann Co., 1926), 223 pages.

Every Child's Garden, A Visitation Nun (St. Louis, Mo.: Academy of the Visitation, 1926), 63 pages.

Externals of the Catholic Church, The, Rev. John Sullivan (New York: Kenedy and Sons, 1918), 385 pages.

First Communion, Mother Mary Loyola (New York: Benziger Bros., 1906), 498 pages.

First Confession, Mother Mary Loyola (New York: Benziger Bros.), 63 pages.

Jesus of Nazareth, Mother Mary Loyola (New York: Benziger Bros., 1917), 401 pages.

Leading the Little Ones to Christ, Rev. George M. Dennerle (Milwaukee: The Bruce Publishing Co., 1932), 305 pages.

Life on Earth of Our Blessed Lord for Little Catholic Children, The, Grace Keon (New York: Kenedy and Sons, 1917), 79 pages.

Little Ones, The, Mary Eaton (St. Louis: B. Herder Book Co., 1925), 151 pages.

Mass, The, Rev. Joseph Dunney (New York: Macmillan Co., 1925), 375 pages.

Practical Aids for Catholic Teachers, Rev. Felix M. Kirsch, O.F.M., and Sister M. Aurelia, O.S.F. (New York: Benziger Bros., 1928), 305 pages.

Teacher Tells a Story, Books I and II (New York: Benziger Bros., 1925), 352 pages.

Teacher's Handbook to the Catechism (3 vols.), Rev. A. Urban (New York: Joseph F. Wagner, Inc.).

Teaching the Ten Commandments, School Sisters of Notre Dame (Milwaukee: The Bruce Publishing Co., 1931), 170 pages.

Tell Us Another, Rev. Wilfrid Herbst (St. Nazianz, Wis.: Salvatorian Fathers, 1925).

To the Heart of the Child, Josephine Van Dyke Brownson (New York: The Encyclopedia Press, Inc., 1917), 193 pages.

RESOURCE LIST

We have collected on the following pages a comprehensive list of all the recommended resources found in this manual. Based on their content and/or their frequent use in this series (often across more than one grade level) we have indicated the most essential of these with an asterisk (*), while resources which may be found on the internet are marked with a cross (†).

First Grade Teacher Resources

*† *The Holy Bible.*

* *Art Education through Religion*, Mary G. McMunigle (New York: Mentzer, Bush & Company, 1931).

† *The Catechism in Examples (5 volumes)*, Rev. D. Chisolm (London: R & T Washbourne, 1919).

* *A Child's Garden of Religion Stories*, Rev. P. Henry Matimore, S.T.D. (New York: The Macmillan Company, 1929).

* *First Communion*, Mother Mary Loyola (London: Burns & Oates, 1896).

* *Jesus of Nazareth: The Story of His Life Written for Children*, Mother Mary Loyola (New York: Benziger Brothers, 1906).

* *Leading the Little Ones to Christ*, Rev. George M. Dennerle (Milwaukee: Bruce Publishing Company, 1932).

† *The Life of Our Lord Written for Little Ones*, Mother Mary Salome (London: Burns And Oates, 1900).

* *The Little Ones: A Course of Relgious Instruction for children up to eight years*, Mary Eaton (London: Sands & Co., 1925).

† *The Lord's Prayer*, Frederick M. Lynk, S.V.D. (Techny: Mission Press, 1915).

Practical Aids for Catholic Teachers, Sr. Mary Aurelia, O.S.F., M.A. and Rev. Felix M. Kirsch, O.M.Cap., Litt.D. (New York: Benziger Brothers, 1928).

Teacher Tells a Story (2 volumes), Rev. Jerome D. Hannan, D.D. (New York: Benziger Brothers, 1925).

† *Teacher's Handbook to the Catechism (3 Volumes)*, Rev. A. Urban (New York: Joseph F. Wagner, 1902).

* *Teaching the Ten Commandments*, S. Mary Agnesine, S. Mary Catherine, SSND (Milwaukee: Bruce Publishing Company, 1931).

* † *To the Heart of the Child*, Josephine Van Dyke Brownson (New York: The Universal Knowledge Foundation, 1918).

The Wonder Days, Marion Ames Taggart (New York: Benziger Brothers, 1923).

First Grade Student Readers

(This list is provided for reference purposes; the majority of recommended readings from these books has been included in a newly published anthology reader to accompany this series.)

The American Cardinal Reader, Primer, Edith M. McLaughlin (New York: Benziger Brothers, 1927).

The American Cardinal Reader, Book One, Edith M. McLaughlin (New York: Benziger Brothers, 1928).

The American Readers for Catholic Schools: Primer, The School Sisters of Notre Dame (Boston: D.C. Heath and Company, 1928).

The American First Reader for Catholic Schools, The School Sisters of Notre Dame (Boston: D.C. Heath and Company, 1928).

Cathedral Basic Readers, Book One, Rev. John A. O'Brien, Ph.D. (Chicago: Scott, Foresman and Company, 1930).

The Catholic Child First Reader, Rena A. Weider, B.S. and Msgr. Charles F. McEvoy, A.M., LL.D. (Chicago: The John C. Winston Company, 1928).

The Corona Readers, Primer, James H. Fassett (Boston: Ginn and Company, 1912).

The Corona Readers, First Reader, James H. Fassett (Boston: Ginn and Company, 1918).

The Ideal Catholic Reader, First Reader, A Sister of St. Joseph (New York: The MacMillan Company, 1915).

Misericordia Readers First Reader, The Sisters of Mercy (Chicago: Rand McNally & Company, 1927).

The Marquette Readers First Reader, The Sisters of Mercy of St. Xavier (New York: The MacMillan Company, 1925).

The Rosary Readers, Primer, Sister Mary Henry, O.S.D. (Boston: Ginn and Company, 1927).

SPECIAL UNIT FOR FIRST HOLY COMMUNION

Teacher Resources

* †*The Holy Bible.*

The Children's Charter, Mother Mary Loyola (New York: Burns And Oates, 1911).

**First Communion,* Mother Mary Loyola (London: Burns And Oates, 1896).

**First Confession,* Mother Mary Loyola (New York: Benziger Brothers, 1902).

Eucharistia, Rev. Joseph Kramp, S.J. (St. Paul: E.M. Lohmann Company, 1926).

Holy Mass, Winfrid Herbst, S.D.S. (New York: Benziger Brothers, 1932).

**The Little Ones: A Course of Relgious Instruction for children up to eight years,* Mary Eaton (London: Sands & Co., 1925).

The Faith for Children (from Seven to Fourteen), Mary Eaton (London: Sands & Co., 1925).

†*Little Talks to Children Preparing for Holy Communion,* Joseph Gummersbach (St. Louis: B. Herder, 1913).

The Mass, Joseph Aloysius Dunney (New York: The MacMillan Company, 1924).

*_Teacher Tells a Story (2 volumes),_ Rev. Jerome D. Hannan, D.D. (New York: Benziger Brothers, 1925).

*_Tell us Another: Sixty-five Charming Stories for Children,_ Winfrid Herbst, S.D.S. (St. Nazianz: The Society of the Divine Savior, 1929).

* †*To the Heart of the Child,* Josephine Van Dyke Brownson (New York: The Universal Knowledge Foundation, 1918).

Externals of the Catholic Church, Rt. Rev. John F. Sullivan (New York: P.J. Kenedy & Sons, 1917).

†*The Visible Church,* Rt. Rev. John F. Sullivan (New York: P.J. Kenedy & Sons, 1920). (*This is a rearrangement of the material found in the author's previous book,* Externals of the Catholic Church.)

Student Readers for First Communion Unit

(As noted previously, most of the recommended reading for this unit found in the books comprising this list have been collected in a newly published anthology reader to accompany this series.)

The American Cardinal Reader, Book Two, Edith M. McLaughlin (New York: Benziger Brothers, 1930).

The American Cardinal Reader, Book Three, Edith M. McLaughlin (New York: Benziger Brothers, 1929).

The American Second Reader for Catholic Schools, The School Sisters of Notre Dame (Boston: D.C. Heath and Company, 1928).

The American Third Reader for Catholic Schools, The School Sisters of Notre Dame (Boston: D.C. Heath and Company, 1928).

Cathedral Basic Readers, Book Three, Rev. John A. O'Brien, Ph.D. (Chicago: Scott, Foresman and Company, 1931).

Columbus Series Third Reading Book, W.T. Vylmen, Ph. D (New York: Schwartz, Kirwin & Fauss, 1899).

The Corona Readers, Book 3, James H. Fassett (Boston: Ginn and Company, 1912).

The Ideal Catholic Reader, Third Reader, A Sister of St. Joseph (New York: The MacMillan Company, 1916).

Misericordia Readers Second Reader, The Sisters of Mercy (Chicago: Rand McNally & Company, 1927).

The Rosary Readers Second Reader, Sister Mary Henry, O.S.D. (Boston: Ginn and Company, 1926).

The Rosary Readers Third Reader, Sister Mary Henry, O.S.D. (Boston: Ginn and Company, 1927).

Additional Student Reading for First Communion Unit

A Child's True Story of Jesus, A Dominican Sister (Chicago: Lawdale Publishing House, 1928).

*A Child's Garden of Religion Stories, Rev. P. Henry Matimore, S.T.D. (New York: The Macmillan Company, 1929).

*Heroes of God's Church, Rev. P. Henry Matimore, S.T.D. (New York: The Macmillan Company, 1930).

*Wonder Stories of God's People, Rev. P. Henry Matimore, S.T.D. (New York: The Macmillan Company, 1929).

*First Communion Days, A Sister of Notre Dame (St. Louis: B. Herder Book Co., 1920).

Hymns for First Communion, Sisters of St. Francis (Dubuque).

My Communion Book, Austin Guildford Schmidt, S.J. (Chicago: Loyola University Press, 1925).

My Happiest Day: True Stories for First Communicants, Rev. Francis A. Reuter (New York: William J. Hirten, 1924).

My Mass Book, Sisters Servants of the IHM (New York: The MacMillan Company, 1929).

*The Mass for Children, Rev. William R. Kelly (New York: Benziger Brothers, 1925).

*Our Sacraments, Rev. William R. Kelly (New York: Benziger Brothers, 1927).

*Our First Communion, Rev. William R. Kelly (New York: Benziger Brothers, 1925).

The Wonder Gifts, Marion Ames Taggart (New York: Benziger Brothers, 1923).

THE HIGHWAY TO HEAVEN SERIES

Prepared in the Catechetical Institute of Marquette University

(In co-operation with a group of Priests and Sisters teaching in the elementary schools)

GRADE	TEXT	MANUAL CURRICULUM IN RELIGION *(1st to 8th Grade inclusive)*
1	**THE BOOK OF THE HOLY CHILD** By *Sister Mary Bartholomew, O.S.F.* 96 pages	First Grade Teachers Plan Book and Manual
2	**THE LIFE OF MY SAVIOR** By a School Sister of Notre Dame 196 pages	Second Grade Teachers Plan Book and Manual
3	**THE LIFE OF THE SOUL** Prepared in the Catechetical Institute of Marquette University *Edward A. Fitzpatrick, Ph.D.* Educational Director 144 pages	Third Grade Teachers Plan Book and Manual
4	**BEFORE CHRIST CAME** By a School Sister of Notre Dame 256 pages	Fourth Grade Teachers Plan Book and Manual
5	**THE VINE AND THE BRANCHES** By the *Rev. R. G. Bandas, Ph.D.Agg., S.T.D. et M.* and a School Sister of Notre Dame 320 pages	Fifth Grade Teachers Plan Book and Manual
6	**THE SMALL MISSAL**	Workbook for the Missal
7 & 8	**THE HIGHWAY TO GOD** Prepared in the Catechetical Institute of Marquette University *Edward A. Fitzpatrick, Ph.D.* Educational Director 420 pages	Practical Problems in Religion By the *Rev. R. G. Bandas, Ph.D.Agg., S.T.D. et M.* (Answers problems in text)

CPSIA information can be obtained
at www.ICGtesting.com
Printed in the USA
BVHW04s1724010918
525798BV00004B/26/P